S0-DLT-119

# The Millennium Countdown

## A PRACTICAL GUIDE TO PREPARING

### YOUR BUSINESS FOR THE

# year2000

## Lynn Craig and Mike Kusmirak

KOGAN
PAGE

**Disclaimer**

All information provided and guidance offered in this book is of a general nature and is not provided with any warranty as to its suitability to the needs of any specific business or organization, but will need to be adapted to the circumstances of each individual business. Readers and users are entirely responsible for taking appropriate action with regard to the Year 2000 issue within their own organizations and for consequences of such actions; the authors and publisher accept no liability whatsoever for any loss or damage which may arise from reliance on anything in this book. Nothing in this book constitutes legal or professional advice. Always consult a properly qualified lawyer, accountant, IT consultant or other professional advisor on any specific problem or matter.

This publication is designed to provide accurate and authoritative information in regard to the subject matter covered. It is sold with the understanding that the publisher is not engaged in rendering legal, accounting, or other professional service. If legal advice or other expert assistance is required, the services of a competent professional person should be sought.

Copyright © 1998 Year 2000 Support Center
All rights reserved. The text of this publication, or any part thereof, may not be reproduced in any manner whatsoever without written permission from the publisher.

Inquiries concerning reproduction outside those terms should be sent to the publishers at the undermentioned address:
Kogan Page Limited
163 Central Ave., Suite 2
Hopkins Professional Building
Dover, New Hampshire 03820

ISBN: 0-7494-2887-2

Cover design by Alicen Brown

Printed in the United States of America
98 99 00 10 9 8 7 6 5 4 3 2

Kogan Page books are available at special quantity discounts to use as premiums and sales promotions, or for use in corporate training programs. For more information, please call the Special Sales Manager at 603-749-9171, or write to Kogan Page, 163 Central Ave., Suite 2, Dover, New Hampshire 03820.

# Contents

# 1. Introduction

As the new century draws nearer and nearer, companies and other commercial organizations are struggling to come to terms with the impact of the Year 2000 computer date problem (popularly known as the "Millennium Bomb," "Millennium Bug," or "Y2K"). There are a number of aspects of this particular crisis that make it unique in modern history.

**It is both dangerous and indiscriminate.** Government experts in the United States and the United Kingdom, the two countries where Year 2000 awareness is most advanced, are of the opinion that businesses which fail to protect themselves are running a real risk of commercial failure. It is clear that firms of all sizes and at all stages of commercial development are at risk; from microfirms with a couple of people working in them, right through to multinationals employing tens of thousands.

*It is also clear that companies can be laid low by the Year 2000 crisis even if they do not have a single computer on the premises.*

No modern business exists in isolation; all rely on a host of other organizations to keep going, including suppliers, banks, the utilities, and, of course, customers. If any of them stumble and fall early in 2000, their failure could bring you down too.

1

**The deadline is absolute.** The vast majority of business projects and problems can endure a little slippage — but not the Year 2000 crisis. "Better late than never" simply does not apply. There will be no second chances.

**The Year 2000 problem CAN BE FIXED.** It is not technically complex, and there are a number of tried and tested solutions available. Any company that addresses the Year 2000 problem resolutely and speedily should be able to protect itself. This book aims to help you do just that.

This book is also designed with the needs of the smaller enterprise in mind. Large commercial organizations have the luxury of being able to siphon resources — managerial, technical and financial — from all parts of the venture. Smaller ventures are just as much at risk, but are not usually able to throw money or people at the problem.

This guide has been written to meet the needs of owner/managers of small firms, and directors of larger companies that do not have full-time Information Technology (IT) staff to help them solve the problem.

It will also prove useful to the leaders of divisions and groups within both private and public sector organizations who find themselves being asked to prepare themselves for the year 2000 without the aid of IT management. Whether you are an owner/operator of a small business with a single elderly computer in the corner, or a medium-sized company with 250 employees using a network of modern PCs and workstations, this book offers you practical guidance, step-by-step, to help sort out your Year 2000 problems.

The issues that need to be addressed tend to fall into two main categories, managerial and technical. This book gives you guidance on the technical areas that need to be examined, and a pretty good idea of whether you can address them yourself, or whether you need to call in help from outside in the form of an IT supplier or consultant.

But throughout, we aim to arm you with enough knowledge to ask the right questions of the "experts." There are a lot of people who are trying to make money from the Year 2000 problem who may know a lot less about it than they claim — and there are also plenty of people who are trying to avoid facing up to the consequences of the problem.

Be suspicious of people who make sweeping statements like, "There is no Year 2000 problem here" or "You needn't worry about that" or "We have the situation under control" — but who cannot then give detailed responses to simple questions like "How do you know?" It is your business that is at risk, and you cannot afford to be shrugged off. You have to know. By the time you finish reading this book, you may find that you know a lot more about the realities of the Year 2000 problem than most of these "experts." Use your knowledge to defend yourself and those who rely on you.

You are welcome to use the material in the guide as a basis for developing and increasing awareness amongst your staff. If you find that outside organizations — typically your customers and suppliers — are unaware of the Year 2000 problem, or are uncertain about how to tackle the issue, let them know about this guide.

The authors accept that guidance which can be taken up by a medium-sized firm with (say) 200 employees will not always be appropriate for a microfirm with a handful of people working in it, and throughout the book, where required, varying guidance is indicated.

# 2. What has caused the Year 2000 problem?

The Year 2000 problem relates to the inability of most computers and computer programs to recognize the transition from 1999 to 2000 in what we would see as "the correct way." Many will work as though the year after 1999 is 1900, or 1980. Some may just stop working. This problem affects not only large mainframe computers and company networks, but also desktop PCs, notebooks and laptop computers, as well as automated equipment and process control equipment controlled by microcontrollers and by "black boxes."

Why? Because most computers have been programmed to think of years as two digits instead of four — so "97" stands for 1997. As midnight strikes on December 31, 1999, these computers will suddenly be faced with a date of "00," and because they have always worked in a 20th century context, they will assume that "00" means 1900, and not 2000.

## 2.1 A problem ignored is a problem stored

Back in the 1960s, when data was input through punched cards, information had to be squeezed into as small a space as possible. Managers worked out that if their programmers wrote a date out using six digits (12/25/69), i.e., using only two digits for the year, they would save 25% of the space they would have needed if they had used the full eight-digit field format of 12/25/1969. Some prescient souls pointed out that this was storing up problems for the future, but this was a fast-moving industry, and people assumed that none of the systems and programs they were working with then would still be in use by the end of the century.

The only problem was that each new generation of programs and systems had to work with existing ones, which were of course written using two-digit year dates — and so the new ones continued to use the same technique. Also, as programs developed over the years, many simply bolted on new sections with new features, leaving the original code at the heart of the program. Throughout the 1970s and 1980s, it was always easier to continue with the existing system than to take the bull by the horns and make the transfer to four digits.

This was also the case with minicomputers, which were introduced in the 1970s. The problem worsened because the authors of software for personal computers (introduced in the 1980s) — although they were aware of the looming Year 2000 problem, and had prepared their software for it — failed to tell users about it. So the users and developers continued in ignorance to use two-digit instead of four-digit date fields, and computers were not programmed to understand that there was a 21st century.

## 2.2 Consequences

So, unless they are fixed, tens of millions of computers and programs will roll over from December 31, 1999, to January 1, 1900. This gives the computer a problem. If it is asked to process a date like 1958 (say a birth date for the purposes of calculating a pension), it is logical for it to assume that 1958 is still 58 years away in the future — the date has not even happened yet. Even if it does not roll over to 1900, it will still not automatically know whether the "58" it has stored means 1958 or 2058. This, as you can imagine, will confuse it.

This phenomenon has already started to cause some problems, giving us a tiny foretaste of things to come. Some credit card readers have refused to recognize expiration dates of the year 2000 and later. Some stores have found that their stock control computers were signaling goods for destruction because they had a sell-by date later than December 1999.

## 2.3 Some "what if" scenarios

**Scenario One:** At the end of January 2000, your bookkeeper tells you that half of your best customers — who normally pay within your usual 30-day credit period — have outstanding balances stretching back into early December. You follow up with them, but they all ask for copies of invoices — and deny any knowledge of the bills. You press them, and they start to come clean — they admit that their accounting systems have been sent into a spin by Year 2000 problems, and they cannot pay you until they sort it out. These are good customers, whom you normally rely upon. Should you go to court, or wait? If you do the former, you'll almost certainly lose them as customers for the future, which is bad for business. If you do the latter, your resulting cash flow problems may put you out of business.

**Scenario Two:** Towards the end of December 1999 you send an order for 100 ABC widgets to a specialized ABC widget maker. The goods are due to be received by you in the third week of January so that you can complete a valuable order for 100 ABC machines in which the ABC widgets are a vital component. The third week of January comes and no ABC widgets appear. You telephone the supplier. He says he has no record of your order on his computerized system. He agrees to produce the goods, but it will take two weeks at least (possibly longer as he has to buy in parts — and his suppliers seem to have some problems at the moment with their computer systems). Your customer is upset at the late delivery, because his contract was based on keeping to a strict timetable, and he makes it plain he won't be giving you any more business. Both you and your customer have lost out because just one company in the customer-supplier chain had a Year 2000 problem.

**Scenario Three:** 1999 was a good year for the firm, and you come to the end of the year with a healthy cash surplus. You decide to place it with a financial institution where you can get a good short-term rate for a couple of months until the money is needed for a contracted project at the end of January 2000. When you try to draw the money out for the project, the institution denies that it has any of your money. You call your accountant, and he confirms that there is no trace of your transaction on their computer system. You have a paper record of the transaction, but sorting out the ensuing wrangle takes a couple of months — during which time you do not have the cash to carry out the original project, and end up being sued for breach of contract.

These are just some of the scenarios that may threaten businesses in 2000. They are not fanciful.

Big business is aware of the threat and is spending billions to sort it out. Small- and medium-sized enterprises need to realize that they are, if anything, even more vulnerable, as they are often at the end of supplier chains and so will feel the ripple effects of any problems further up the chain. In addition, if there are problems with cash flow and interruptions in the routine of order-supply-payment, large companies with deep pockets can just shrug them off as temporary hitches — but smaller organizations may find them absolutely lethal.

All of which means that you MUST take action to ensure that your own computer systems are clear of Year 2000 problems; and that you MUST take action to ensure that your suppliers and customers are not going to cause you problems come the Year 2000. This guide is designed to help you take this action NOW. **You must act now— and here's why.**

# 3. From denial to action

Many businesspeople, directors and managers go through a number of phases before they finally get to grips with the Year 2000 problem. They go something like this:

**Phase One:** They deny that the problem exists at all.

**Tell-tale statements:** *"It's all a myth invented by the computer industry to generate trade."*
*"Someone will write a piece of software to get us over it. Relax."*

**Phase Two:** They accept that the Year 2000 is a headache — but for other people, not them.

**Tell-tale statements:** *"It's only big businesses with mainframe systems that have to worry."*
*"We only use PCs, so we're OK."*

**Phase Three:** They accept that they have a Year 2000 problem, but fail to appreciate that it's *their* problem as managers of the business.

**Tell-tale statements:** *"We've got a bright employee in accounting who gets all the computer magazines, and she's working on it."*
*"I've sent a memo to the Board. That should cover my back."*

**Phase Four:** They realize that this is a serious management issue of the highest order that requires action NOW.

**Tell-tale statements:**   *"Call a staff meeting. We're going to have to get everybody involved in this one."*

*"This is the number one problem to solve for my business — because if I don't solve it, there might not be a business left to worry about."*

## 3.1   Is there a software engineer in the house?

The Year 2000 is most dangerous to your organization while you or your bosses are still going through Phases One to Three. It is not until you get to Phase Four that you can actually start dealing with the problem effectively.

However, the closer we get to December 31, 1999, the more business managers will reach Phase Four — and the greater the demand will be for IT engineers and consultants. After all, there are only so many qualified computer professionals available, and as the inexorable deadline draws closer, those with plenty of money (i.e., big business) will be able to monopolize the available experts. If you need a consultant, you need him or her NOW — because you may not be able to afford that person in a few months' time. (Think of the problem after a severe freeze, and then a thaw. Everyone wants competent plumbers to fix the burst pipes — but there aren't enough to go round. And suddenly every plumber is charging triple overtime.)

## 3.2   My neighbor's problem is my problem

The other reason to act now is that some organizations that you depend upon may need more time than you to sort out their Year 2000 problems.

For example, suppose your firm's best customer is a large manufacturing firm with extensive computer systems. With the help of this book, you might be able to sort out your own problems in a few weeks. But, reading the relevant sections of this guide, you realize that all this good work will be in vain if your number one customer takes a dive — and so you start a campaign to wake up its top management to the problem. Once that happens, the firm takes an inventory and announces that it will take 18 months to sort out all their problems. If this revelation occurs in January 1998, you're probably OK. If it occurs in January 1999, your customer (and you too!) is in big trouble. So the earlier you can start working on your business partners, the better.

## 3.3  Outsiders will expect you to be taking action

Another pressing reason for starting to sort out your Year 2000 problems now is that sooner or later outsiders are going to come knocking on your door to ask what you are doing about the situation. If you are able to give them a prompt and detailed answer showing how you assessed the problem and took the right steps to solve or contain it, you will satisfy them. If, on the other hand, you cannot give them convincing answers, there will be a large question mark hanging over your firm in the eyes of those outsiders, with possible damaging consequences.

They will want to know whether you have:

- Seriously considered whether you have a problem;
- Carried out an inventory (listing) of all your computer systems and software;
- Used the information from that inventory to see how those systems fit into your business, so that you can establish which systems are the most critical for the success and survival of your business;
- Analyzed those systems for date problems;
- Fixed, or have planned how to fix, any date problems that have been discovered;
- Tested all systems and interfaces thoroughly;

■ Checked, or have a plan to check, the compliance status of suppliers and customers; and

■ Prepared a contingency plan to cover any circumstances that may arise if you cannot fix all the date problems in your systems (leaving plenty of time for detailed testing) by December 31, 1999, or if your suppliers or customers have problems which are going to rebound on you.

This list may seem pretty daunting right now— but this book will tell you how to go about completing all the steps described above.

These outsiders include:

### Your customers

More and more companies are writing to their suppliers asking whether they are going to be able to provide an uninterrupted supply of goods and services after December 31, 1999. This process started early in 1997 with some very large companies and some of the supermarket giants, but undoubtedly more and more companies of all sizes are going to start asking their suppliers hard questions. When you receive one of these letters, you cannot afford to ignore it and still expect that customer to have confidence in you as a trusted supplier. You may feel upset that the customer is "poking their nose" into your business — but remember, all they are trying to do is protect *their* business. Give customers the answers they require, or, if you feel the provision of that information would be unreasonable (because it is private or too much) then discuss the matter with them. Treat this matter as sufficiently important to be dealt with by a senior person. And do not say that you have dealt with your Year 2000 issues when the truth is that you have hardly started. Your customer may ask you to back up your statements with facts — for example the written results of the tests on your systems for Year 2000 compliance. The customer will probably be selecting their suppliers from those that give them the right answers promptly; but what the customer is looking for is an awareness of the problem and a plan for dealing with it in plenty of time. All of which means that you should start working on the Year 2000 problem NOW.

## Your bank

Bankers are in business too, and part of their business is not lending money to companies that are a bad risk. A company that is not preparing itself for the Year 2000 definitely qualifies as a bad risk! Obviously, your bank's expectations of you are going to be different as time goes on. In 1998 a typical banker or lender will expect you to have developed an awareness of the Year 2000 problem, and to have begun making plans on how you are going to tackle it. By autumn 1999, the same banker or lender will expect you to have completed (or almost completed) any testing of systems required, and to have a well-considered contingency plan in place. If you fail to meet his or her expectations, why should the bank lend you money or extend overdraft facilities to you? On a more positive note, you should understand that your bank has *a real interest in ensuring your survival* — after all, you are a customer, and nobody wants their customers to fail in droves come the Year 2000. Do not be afraid of asking your bank for help and advice. If, in the process of carrying out your Year 2000 work, you discover you need to replace systems or employ consultants and need more funding, you are likely to get a sympathetic hearing.

## Insurance companies

Your insurers have an interest in what you are doing about the Year 2000, particularly as it relates to business risks liability. If your business suffered loss because it had not prepared itself properly for the Year 2000, the insurance company might not pay out. Some insurers have said that any business that neglects to upgrade its computer systems before the end of 1999 risks losing its insurance coverage against a loss stemming from computer failure. This potentially involves not just coverage against the interruption to business caused by loss of data such as customer records, but also insurance against fire and theft. If computerized security systems failed to work because policyholders had neglected to deal with their millennium problem, insurers may refuse to pay subsequent claims. You may not be able to get coverage under directors' and officers' liability insurance if the insurer thinks your company has not started to take action in time.

## Other regulatory authorities

Many businesses are regulated by statutory agencies and bodies. These businesses are expected to keep proper records and to deliver regular reports of their performance and compliance with certain standards. Failure to keep those records properly and to deliver accurate reports may result in the closing or suspension of the whole or part of the business. Serious problems could arise in these areas if your data recording systems fail to work correctly after December 31, 1999. Businesses affected could include those that are subject to environmental restrictions, as well as those in banking and insurance, where a corrupted client database could result in the giving of bad advice.

## Auditors

Your auditors will also become interested in what you are doing about the Year 2000. Their needs are generally to check and report on whether your financial accounting and reporting system is adequate. If it is going to handle the 2000 date incorrectly, it probably isn't adequate. They also have to report on whether your business is a "going concern." If your computer systems are likely to malfunction after 1999, your auditors may conclude that the business is unlikely to remain a going concern for very long. If they come up with negatives on these points the auditors will have to qualify their audit report to your accounts. This would be seen by your bank and any of your creditors who examine your accounts, and this might have an adverse effect on your ability to trade.

## Guidance for smaller firms

Even if the law does not require you to undergo a formal audit, you may come under pressure to produce evidence of an audit of some kind or some other proof that a professional accountant has examined your business for its Year 2000 viability.

## 3.4 Get your priorities clear

In summary, to meet all the requirements of your business and the demands of others, including legal responsibilities, you must take action NOW to keep your business healthy. Make sure you keep detailed records of all actions taken to deal with all Year 2000 problems — you may be asked to supply proof in the event of legal or regulatory action. Consider these business priorities:

**You need customers:**    Prove to them that you will still be in business after 1999

**You need suppliers:**    Help them get on top of their own Year 2000 problems

**You need funding:**    Give the bank confidence that you will sort out your Year 2000 problems in good time

**You need to keep on the right side of the law:**    Ensure that you can meet the requirements of regulatory authorities, and that you fulfill your business' commitments

**You need insurance coverage:**    Make sure that your Year 2000 actions are prompt and thorough or you may face soaring premiums or a withdrawal of coverage altogether

**You need credibility:**    Don't pass your business off as Year 2000 compliant if it's not. But get to work on it right away!

But it's not all bad news. You may also find that tackling the Year 2000 issue vigorously and quickly may produce some unexpected benefits:

■ Your company may win a competitive edge over its less well-prepared rivals;

■ You may win new customers and raise your status to that of key supplier for your existing clients; and

■ By helping your suppliers and customers through the Year 2000 crisis, you may well forge closer and more productive working relationships.

# 4. Where are problems likely to arise?

## 4.1 Computer systems

This is the most obvious area of the business where you will have problems. You will find a list of the areas in the business in which you might use computers contained in Appendix Five.

This guide will take you through the steps needed to check if your systems and software are affected by the Year 2000 problem, and what you should do about it.

## 4.2 Telephone systems

It is unlikely that any business would survive if its telephone system went out of operation for more than a week or so. You would not be able to communicate with your customers and suppliers. It is essential to check with your supplier whether your own telephone system will function without problems before, during and after January 1, 2000. We suggest you insist on getting a statement in writing from your supplier, particularly as some unscrupulous salespeople trying to sell you a new system between now and 2000 may suggest that your existing system is not compliant when, in fact, it is.

You should be aware that even if your own telephone system works correctly, there may be problems in making and completing calls to overseas destinations, due to possible problems with overseas telephone companies.

## 4.3  Transmitting data

You may currently transmit data to or from financial organizations, suppliers, customers and other people outside your computer system. You may do this from your computer, whether over normal telephone lines or by ISDN. Typical areas of online data transfer are sending data to your bank, using a credit card terminal or ATM, and sending orders to, or receiving them from, your wholesaler, supplier or customer.

You may also transmit data carried on floppy disk, on one of the various large storage formats (e.g., Zip, Jazz or SyQuest), or on tape. Typically these might include mailing lists going to a fulfillment house, databases containing customer and ordering information, or artwork. Any or all of these data transmission types may also occur within your business.

If one of your trading partners transmits data to you which does not recognize the Year 2000, this could cause problems. Similarly, if they correctly transmit data that your system does not recognize (i.e., it treats it as 1900 data — not 2000 data) there are going to be problems.

Consider the possibility of a customer (whose system is Year 2000 compliant) sending you an order which your computer doesn't recognize. The customer's production line may come to a standstill waiting for you to fulfill the order, and you may be paying your staff to hang around waiting for an order which you think hasn't arrived.

## 4.4  Suppliers

The survival of your suppliers is vital to you, especially if they are responsible for products, parts or services you would find difficult to obtain from others. For this reason, you will have a great interest in making certain that they are actively dealing with Year 2000 matters in their organizations. And they, for their part, should be interested in what action you are taking as their customer. They want to receive orders and be paid. So it will benefit both of you to start talking about this matter.

If you get a negative or inadequate response from a vital supplier, start hunting for an alternative source of supply quickly. Your existing supplier may not be around for much longer.

## 4.5   The utilities

You are dependent upon the utilities for the continued supply of basic services to your business; these include electricity and telephones for all businesses, and many firms also need a continued supply of gas and/or water to keep their production processes going.

Without power, you can't heat or light your premises, run your production systems, and certainly cannot run your computers; without telephone lines you cannot communicate to the outside world either using voice or data. If transport systems don't work properly, you will be unable to get your staff to work or ship out your goods.

We recommend you send letters to the manager of each of your utility service suppliers, and keep the pressure on until you are satisfied that there will be no interruption to the service after December 31, 1999.

## 4.6   Customers

No customers, no business. Their survival is vital to you. But even if your customers get through the early months of 2000 without actually going bust, you might find that they are so disrupted by trying to cope with Year 2000 problems that their normal activities —

like placing fresh orders with you, or paying you the money they owe — may go by the board.

You need to talk to your customers about all this, and you need to help each other through this difficult period.

If your business relies very heavily on just one or two customers, it is a good idea to start trying to broaden your customer base. Certainly, if one of your most important customers refuses to accept that there is a Year 2000 issue at all, you should take account in your business planning of the possibility that that customer will not be trading after 1999. If you usually extend long credit to such customers, start to reduce the terms now; try to go into the new millennium without being owed money by these people. You may never see it again.

One other point to take note of in relation to customers is that if, after December 31, 1999, you fail to deliver the goods and services that you are contractually obliged to deliver, you may leave yourself open to legal action. So you may want to change your own Terms of Business to cope with any business interruption. Check with your legal adviser.

## 4.7 Embedded systems and automated processes

In the long run, Year 2000 problems associated with automated equipment may prove a bigger headache than noncompliant computers. Much of this equipment uses microcontrollers to control its actions. Some of these microcontrollers are designed to be aware of the date, because they need to switch on and off at specified times, or so that maintenance cycles can be observed. Other systems do not need to use date-aware chips, but have them installed anyway simply because it was cheaper for the manufacturer to supply all its chips as such.

Equipment that relies on the proper functioning of date-related actions may cause problems in 2000. Other equipment may shut down automatically and unexpectedly because, although it does not normally need to take account of the date, it contains a chip that has suddenly found itself faced with "00" as a date.

So you may find, for example, that if your security system keeps the building locked on Saturdays and Sundays, you are locked out of your building on the morning of Thursday, January 6, 2000.

Why? Because a microcontroller with a Year 2000 problem thinks that it is actually January 6, 1900 — which was a Saturday.

You may also find that equipment which is controlled by automated systems will simply shut down. At one end of the spectrum, if the heating goes on the blink in early January, things might get rather chilly for you and your staff. At the other end, critical safety systems may malfunction, putting people's lives in danger.

Other equipment may provide incorrect data to systems whose actions then become erratic (i.e., equipment that should be turned on, turns off and vice versa), or incorrect data may be reported, and this could lead to a closure by regulatory authorities (i.e., in relation to environmental problems, whether with a power station or a farm).

Some items of equipment have the microcontroller(s) embedded in their systems. Others have a dedicated computer attached which controls the equipment. Machines that might be affected include fax machines, production equipment, distribution equipment, elevators, security systems, etc. In Appendix Six we explain more about the nature of embedded systems, and give more detailed lists of equipment that might be affected. Section 18 contains some practical steps for you to consider.

## 4.8 Companies selling computer systems and automated equipment

Where you supply computer systems and/or automated equipment in the course of your business, you will have legal liability for what you supply and this may include liability for any problems to your customer's businesses that may be caused if the equipment fails after December 31, 1999. You may also incur liability under health and safety legislation.

## 4.9 Liability to third parties

You should also be aware that you may incur liabilities to third parties beyond the normal supplier/customer relationship. For example, if an elevator in your building malfunctioned while carrying visitors, you might find yourself liable should they be injured.

## 4.10 Business premises and facilities

Where you operate out of premises and have a responsibility for staff, you will need to check that the following will not have any problems at the turn of the century:

■ Security systems and environment controls (e.g., heating, air-conditioning, fire alarms, drainage); and
■ General facilities (e.g., elevators, telephone exchanges, etc.).

These need checking to protect the security of your business and the safety of your staff, customers and the public. These are automated systems and may be driven by "embedded" microcontrollers which may have a Year 2000 date problem (see Section 4.7 and Chapter 18, and the Appendix Six).

Check every piece of automated equipment you use, in the office, in the factory or warehouse, or on the road (cars and vans). They should be included in your inventory (see Section 10.7). Contact both the manufacturers and suppliers (the suppliers may not have enough information) and get written confirmation from their senior (technical) management as to the problems that might arise, if any. Do not rely on verbal assurances, and (regrettably) do not rely on the word of sales or marketing personnel. If you are not responsible for the provision of the above because you rent or lease your business premises, you must ask your building landlord or other relevant owner to check the position regarding all building systems. If you work out of a business center, you may need to check services provided, such as common accounting facilities, etc.

# 5. What you need to do now — an action checklist

## 5.1 Clear the decks

Before you do anything else, you must ensure that you do not buy any new hardware or software unless it is Year 2000 compliant. You must also make sure that all new computer services or consultancy you buy from now on have a Year 2000 compliance clause in your favor. See Appendix Two for contractual advice.

## 5.2 Put someone in charge

The next thing to do is to put someone in charge of your firm's Year 2000 project. (See Section 10.1 for details.)

### Guidance for smaller firms

This will almost certainly be the owner/manager— for microfirms, he or she usually represents the sole managerial resource available. We know that you are hard-pressed and have a thousand other things to think about, but you must make time to tackle this issue head-on. It's your business and your future — so take charge.

In a partnership, either take joint responsibility for the Year 2000 problem, and carve up the work between you, or decide which of you is going to handle it. You must be prepared to spend money if it is needed, and to support each other.

### Guidance for larger firms

You need to appoint a senior member of the business as the Year 2000 project manager. There are strong arguments for making it the responsibility of the managing director or chief executive. This person will need to have full authority to turn the business upside down, and to make hard decisions about spending and resources.

Regardless of the size of your firm, you need to involve all the employees in the Year 2000 project. After all, they are stakeholders in the business too — if it goes under, they are out of a job. In dealing with the Year 2000 problem, it is essential that nothing is missed, and that you cover every angle.

For the larger firm, getting the staff involved may mean timetabling a series of regular meetings to exchange ideas and report on progress. The smaller firm can be more informal, but should be no less stringent in keeping everybody working together.

### 5.3 The checklist

■ **Carry out an internal inventory.** You must draw up a complete and detailed list of the equipment in your business. This includes:
- Hardware;
- Software;
- Automated/embedded systems; and
- Interfaces between all of the above.

You will find information on how to do this in Section 10.7, and sample inventory forms can be obtained from The Year 2000 Support Center — see page 93 for details.

■ **Carry out an external inventory.** You need to draw up a complete list of all the ways in which your systems link up with outside bodies, and how you exchange information and data. You will find information on how to do this in Section 15. At the same time, you should start to assess how the outside bodies you have regular dealings with are going to cope with the Year 2000 problem — and what is the likely impact on your business. These will include:

- Your customers;
- Your suppliers of goods and services;
- The utility suppliers (electricity, phone, gas and water);
- Transport providers (who get your staff to work, carry your goods, etc.);
- Your landlord;
- The suppliers of computer systems; and
- The suppliers of automated equipment/embedded systems.

This process of communicating with outside bodies is likely to take some time, so it should continue in parallel with the following steps.

■ **Use the inventories to make a map of connections.** Establish exactly how information and data flows around your business and between your business and external organizations. You may find it helpful to do this in the form of a diagram.

■ **Prioritize.** You need to understand which of the various systems and interfaces you have mapped out are absolutely vital to the survival of your business — "mission-critical" — and which are not (see Section 10.8). Use this priority list to establish which systems and links you need to make Year 2000 compliant first.

■ **Assess the size of your problem.** This will be a mixture of preliminary testing (see Section 19 for guidance on how to do this) and writing to software authors and suppliers of hardware/embedded systems asking for confirmation of compliance status. If the results of these exercises show that you have Year 2000 technical problems, you must decide for each system/item whether to:

| | |
|---|---|
| REPAIR IT | Work on it until it is made compliant |
| REPLACE IT | Opt for an upgraded (and compliant!) version or system, or switch to another way of doing things |

SCRAP IT          Scrap any system which no longer has a useful life (see Section 10.11).

■ **Decide if you need outside help.** Does your firm have the technical resources to deal with some of the items itself? (See Section 10.4 for guidance on how to decide this.) If not, you will need to appoint a suitably qualified and competent IT consultant to assist (see Section 10.6 for guidance on how to go about this).

■ **Set a preliminary budget.** You cannot do this until you have completed the steps above, when you will have an idea of how extensive your problem is likely to be, and whether you will need outside help.

SMALLER FIRMS    The budget will vary depending on how big your technical problems are. You may find that all that is needed is your time. If on the other hand you have several noncompliant PCs and applications, you will need to work out how much it will cost you to upgrade or replace hardware and software (see Section 10.2).

LARGER FIRMS     You are more likely to have to call in outside help, especially if you have an extensive PC network, a number of electronic interfaces with outside bodies, or use a lot of custom applications (see Section 13).

■ **Do the fixes.** This means either modifying the program code, or selecting and installing the upgraded versions or systems, or setting up new ways of working to get around identified problems. It is sensible once you have started doing this to check how your preliminary budget allocation is shaping up against reality. You may need to allocate more resources in the light of experience.

■ **Test, test and test again.** This is a crucial stage. You must test all your systems and applications and processes thoroughly and in conjunction with each other — but without letting this process flow over into the "live" environment of the day-to-day running of the business (see Section 19 for details). You MUST be sure that there are no errors, and MUST be sure that everything will work once it goes "live."

■ **Go live!** With careful monitoring, you can now set all your newly-compliant systems in place, and use them to run the business. It is not until you get to this stage that you can truthfully say that all your business's systems have been successfully tested for Year 2000 compliance. (Of course, you may still have Year 2000 troubles with your suppliers and customers, the so-called "chain of pain.")

■ **Set up a contingency plan.** Once you have carried out your inventory, and in parallel with the other steps given above, you need to prepare for the unexpected. If you still have doubts about how well your outside partners are going to cope with the Year 2000 — or you realize that you cannot complete all your own Year 2000 corrections in good time — work out how you might get by without them should the worst happen. If you realize that you are not going to be able to resolve all your problems in time, you will need to jump straight to this step and start planning, while continuing to complete the other steps above (see Section 20 for details on establishing a contingency plan).

# 6. How do I know when something is Year 2000 compliant?

Before you can go around telling people that your systems are Year 2000 compliant, you need to have a thorough understanding of what that actually means. By the same token, you need to be sure that you can ask people the right questions if they try to tell you that something (usually a piece of equipment they're trying to sell you or avoid fixing if you bought it earlier) is "Year 2000 compliant."

Compliance means, in broad terms, that a piece of hardware or software, or a system, will function as specified and without interruption, *before, during and after* the transition from December 31, 1999, to January 1, 2000. This means that it will not cause any disruption whatsoever to your business, your employees, your subcontractors, your suppliers, your customers, etc. Moreover, that it will do so "out-of-the-box," i.e., it will function correctly without you having to open the box or play around with the software.

Although it originated in the U.K., the British Standards Institution has provided one of the clearest definitions of Year 2000 Conformity Requirements. This definition is widely used in this country and internationally. In brief, the definition is:

> *Year 2000 conformity shall mean that neither performance nor functionality is affected by dates prior to, during and after the year 2000.*

*In particular:*

*Rule 1.*   *No value for current date will cause any interruption in operation.*

*Rule 2.*   *Date-based functionality must behave consistently for dates prior to, during and after year 2000.*

*Rule 3.*   *In all interfaces and data storage, the century in any date must be specified either explicitly or by unambiguous algorithms or inferencing rules.*

*Rule 4.*   *Year 2000 must be recognized as a leap year.*

Computer companies may use terms such as "Year 2000 ready" or "Year 2000 safe" and even a bland reference to "compliance" — but we suggest there is only ONE statement you can accept, and it must be in writing from someone in authority:

> *This product (if used in accordance with the information in the manual and help files) will not cause any disruption whatsoever to your business, employees, subcontractors, suppliers, customers, etc., before, during and after the period 31 December 1999 and 1 January 2000, and it conforms to the British Standards Institution Definition of Year 2000 Conformity Requirements.*

You should require that any supplier of products or services confirms in writing (signed by an officer or responsible manager from the supplier company) that their products or services conform to this definition.

You may find it useful to look at the sample Year 2000 compliance agreement included in Appendix Two and the Sample Year 2000 Vendor Certification Questionnaire included in Appendix Four.

# 7. Things to remember when buying new hardware and software

It may come as a shock to learn that many items of computer hardware and software being sold today are still not Year 2000 compliant—despite the fact that the IT industry has been talking seriously about this issue since the early 1990s. Plainly, it is reckless to buy any hardware, software, or equipment containing embedded systems without making sure that it is Year 2000 compliant.

First, you should grill the supplier, using the information contained in this guide, to make sure that he or she is promising that the goods are Year 2000 compliant, and that the supplier really understands what that means. Second, get it confirmed in writing, as described in Section Six.

Third, test it anyway! And tell the supplier at the time they are making their promises that you intend to test for compliance. The supplier may start to backtrack when they realize that you are in earnest and know what you are talking about. (See Section 19 for more information on testing.)

This may seem tedious and long-winded, but it is for your own protection. Do not believe manufacturers, suppliers, dealers or salesmen who tell you "It will work. No problem." Be suspicious — it is your business that is at risk.

# 8. Creating awareness of the problem

## 8.1  You need to spread the word ...

The effects of the Year 2000 problem will be felt by most businesses in the world, directly or indirectly. Even if a company doesn't use computers at all, it will almost certainly deal with companies and organizations that do.

So dealing with your own problems is only a first step (although a vital one); you have also to be concerned about other people's problems. It is IN YOUR INTEREST to spread awareness of the Year 2000 problem among all those you have business dealings with. You need to raise their awareness. Making people aware is the first vital step in dealing with the problem.

## 8.2  ... but do it tactfully!

Outsiders may well resent it if you question them about what they feel is literally their own business. So you need to use tact and diplomacy, and to apply pressure gradually. Large conglomerates may be able to issue peremptory letters to their suppliers saying that they must become compliant within the next month or lose their business — but the rest of us need to stay on good terms with our business partners.

Remember that all business is a two-way transaction; to a greater or lesser extent, each of your business partners values their relationship with you. If you can show your partners that you have spent money and time sorting out your own Year 2000 problems, and are ready to help them with advice and guidance on how they can do the same — and indicate, however tactfully, that you think they are in real danger of going under should they ignore you — they should start to listen. Section Nine contains hints and tactics in dealing with this matter.

It makes sense for you to use direct contact as well as letters, and such contact should be made by knowledgeable and respected personnel in the firm, preferably either those who are well-known to the customer or supplier, or the most senior person available — the owner/manager in smaller firms, or the managing director or chairman of larger companies. This is not a job to delegate to a junior person. It may even be helpful to make formal presentations about the Year 2000 to your key customers and suppliers. Again, the Sources of Help section contains details of awareness slide shows that you may find useful.

If you have difficulty getting answers out of customers, you can keep an eye on their Year 2000 preparedness by checking their financial statements. Read their Quarterly and Annual Reports including Notes and the Auditor's Report.

Customers overseas (where there may be less Year 2000 awareness) are much harder to check. If you think things don't look good, you should check your credit insurance cover, or reduce your reliance on giving credit without collateral. Try to make certain you are not too reliant on one customer (don't assume that because they are a "large" company they are not going to have any problems).

## 8.3  Don't forget your own people

Making people inside your business aware of the Year 2000 problem is vital too, because you need them all — from the highest levels of management right down to the most wet-behind-the-ears mailroom clerk — to work with you to beat the problem. Raising their awareness will help them help you. After all, these are the people who are most familiar with the day-to-day operations of the firm; you may have command of the broad picture, but the devil is in the detail, and these people know the details inside out.

You need them to be alert to Year 2000 problems, and to come up with ideas on how to beat them or work around them. You need to encourage flexible thinking and sharpness, because the months leading up to the millennium is inevitably going to be a period of rapid change. You also need them to understand that preparing for the Year 2000 might result in funds being no longer available for other treasured projects.

This is easily done in a small firm with a handful of employees, where all of you can become personally involved in different aspects of the project. Raising internal awareness in larger firms, where you start to get different departments and shifts, is more problematic.

## Guidance for Larger Firms

As we go through the last months prior to January 1, 2000, you will find more and more support materials become available to help you raise awareness in the workplace. These are likely to include videos, leaflets and books like this one. Distributing this book, and the support material included in the Sources of Help section, goes a long way. But informing by paper is not always enough.

Although you may place notices on the notice board and send information to staff in paper form or electronically, getting staff cooperation and understanding should be done face-to-face, whether in groups or individually. In dealing with the Year 2000, your employees are an asset. Use their eyes and ears and brains.

There are a number of ways you can involve your employees and raise their awareness of the Year 2000 issue:

- Get all your managers up to speed with a series of managerial briefings. Use printed notes for reference, or copy relevant sections from this book;
- Hold departmental briefings, preferably led by your managers;
- Involve as many of your staff as possible in the inventory stage. Even nontechnical employees may be able to play a part in some of the testing routines, under the supervision of your IT consultant;
- Encourage useful feedback and input by holding regular sessions in groups or by department. If you keep people well-informed and feeling involved, they are more likely to respond. Don't be afraid to let them know the scale of the problems the company faces: putting a brave face on things and concealing the true state of affairs may just result in your staff not rising to the challenge — as they might if they understand that they are helping to safeguard their own jobs.

One thing that comes out of Year 2000 work is that a much greater discipline needs to be enforced as to the use of hardware and software in many companies. Standards need to be set so that PC software with weak security features is not allowed— corruption of your systems affects the livelihood of all people in the firm. You may wish to review your personnel contracts to deal with employees who do not wish to comply with these standards and introduce noncompliant software into the workplace.

# 9. Contacting suppliers and customers

## 9.1　Get to the right person

Throughout this guide, we stress the need to contact your suppliers and customers about the Year 2000 problem. When you issue letters, you should be seeking a detailed answer to a specific inquiry. It is therefore important to find the individual within the company who can give that response. In larger firms where you may not be aware of all the links between your business and outside organizations, get your managers to draw up lists of key companies with the names of their normal contacts and the CEO.

In most cases, we suggest starting at the top with letters to the managing director or chief executive, signed by the head of your company, or the firm's owner/manager or proprietor.

Don't feel bashful or foolish when you do this; however small your own company, and however large the organization to which you are writing, there is one very important consideration in your mind when you write your letter — the survival of your business. The target organization needs to be aware that this consideration is uppermost in your mind, and you should not be afraid to assert your right to detailed information. If you get shrugged off with a bland, meaningless reply (e.g., "Dear Sir/Madam, Thank you for your inquiry about the Year 2000. I can assure you that we are taking appropriate measures. Yours sincerely etc."), then write back demanding a properly detailed response.

## 9.2 You need proper answers to serious questions

As 2000 draws nearer, a well-run organization (note this for your own company when customers ask you these questions) will prepare an open and honest statement about its Year 2000 preparedness, which should cover all the points that could be reasonably asked, such as:

- Will your business be viable after December 31, 1999, i.e., will you be able to supply goods and services to us without interruption?
- If not, what are you doing to achieve Year 2000 viability, and when do you expect to achieve it?
- Have you checked the viability status of your own suppliers?
- Have you checked the compliance status of your links with your data partners?

If you get no response at all, don't be afraid to telephone and find out why. Keep calling the organizations until you do get the sort of reply you need to satisfy yourself that their businesses are going to remain viable.

If all your efforts are in vain, then you should adjust your business plans on the basis that THE ORGANIZATION MAY WELL GO OUT OF BUSINESS come the Year 2000. If it is a supplier, start looking for an alternative (viable!) source of supply. If it is a customer, you need to reduce your reliance upon them by finding new customers, and by gradually reducing their credit terms so that you do not go into January 2000 with unpaid bills still in their accounts department. If you are carrying out work for them that will straddle the crucial period, ask for payment upfront — and explain why you are doing so. They may be offended and take their work elsewhere — but you must weigh that risk against ending up with an unrecovered debt and a major cash flow nightmare.

## 9.3   You may have to get tough with the utilities

The above approach obviously will not work when dealing with monopoly (or near-monopoly) services such as the utilities. For example, if there is only one water company in town, and they refuse to respond, the only way you may be able to get their attention is by asking a lawyer to force a reply from them. Is this drastic step worth taking? It depends. Some businesses may depend utterly on a continued supply of the water service, for example, if they need water for cooling or washing processes. For them, a failure by the water company to cope with the Year 2000 would result in their own failure. So the real question is, are you prepared to stick your head in the sand and pray that they know what they are doing?

There are ways you can increase the likelihood of getting a sensible response from them without bankrupting yourself. Hunt around among other companies in the area who are in the same boat as you, and join forces. Not only will this distribute costs, but it will improve your "pester power." One small company writing letters may seem like a minor irritation — but if the letter is signed by a dozen companies, even the most resistant of service providers may start to feel uneasy.

Another way to "punch above your weight" is to get your congressional representative involved — he or she is most unlikely to want to see businesses closing in the constituency — and to complain to the relevant industry regulators.

## 9.4   Your campaign should have focus

A mailing campaign should focus on companies whose failure to supply could bring your business to a halt; could cause it substantial problems in its operations; or could cause problems to employees which might mean that they will not be available for work.

It is possible that you do not need to chase all the others if you feel confident that there are sufficient alternative sources of supply. However, don't forget that many suppliers get their products from one or two main manufacturers, and if those manufacturers suddenly have problems, then so will all the suppliers. It may be worthwhile doing a little detective work to find out just how many real alternatives you have.

A major plank in your campaign should be the questioning of the manufacturers of your computer hardware and software to discover whether your systems are Year 2000 compliant or not. Use the questions and techniques described in Sections Six and Seven.

## 9.5    And don't forget the paperwork

Finally, it is vital to keep proper records of your letter-writing campaign, with a log of the responses received, an assessment of whether those responses were deemed adequate, and details of your subsequent actions. Keep these records on paper with your other Year 2000 documents. Why? Because these records help show that you have carried out all reasonable actions to ensure your own company's business viability after December 31, 1999.

# 10. Getting on top of your own problems

## 10.1 Appointing a Year 2000 project manager

You will need to appoint an overall Year 2000 project manager from within your business. In a smaller firm, this will usually be the owner/manager or one of the partners. In a larger firm, this will usually need to be a senior person, with full responsibility, authority and budget (see Section 10.2) to carry out the work needed. This person is someone who:

- Understands your business inside and out;
- Has a good grasp of the computer technology used in the business without necessarily being a computer expert;
- Is a good communicator and a good listener, with the ability to spot good ideas;
- Is respected and able to maintain staff morale; and
- Is able to manage successfully projects with very tight deadlines.

The Year 2000 project manager faces a number of tasks. He or she has to:

- Communicate WHY action has to be taken;
- Establish WHAT action has to be taken;
- Decide by WHOM it has to be taken;
- Decide WHEN it has to be completed; and
- MONITOR everything very carefully.

In larger firms, the Year 2000 project manager needs to set up a team spanning the various departments in the business to carry out the nontechnical tasks set out in this guide. In firms of all sizes, he or she may also need to call upon the support of the firm's external advisers, such as accountants and lawyers.

## 10.2 Setting a budget

The firm able to handle all its Year 2000 problems without spending any money at all is fortunate indeed — and pretty rare.

Even where no actual cash is spent, you will find that management time is taken up with solving the problem, and that this will inevitably carry a price elsewhere in the business. Most firms will find it prudent to set aside funds to cover a number of costs, including some or all of the following:

■ Internal staff costs (e.g., overtime, hiring temporary staff to provide cover) — consider whether retired employees can help out;
■ External consultants, if they are needed, to help create your Year 2000 strategy and to repair your systems should you choose to do so;
■ The costs of audit to supply proof of compliance and viability;
■ Professional fees, for example, audit costs to check compliance, legal fees (checking contracts, pursuing suppliers of faulty equipment), or the costs involved in preparing business contingency plans;
■ Any upgrades or replacement of hardware and software, and new maintenance and support agreements; and
■ Stationery costs — redesigned invoices, statements, etc., which are produced with four-digit dates and not two.

All of which begs the question— how much? This is extremely difficult to estimate, as every business's needs and situation will vary.

As a very rough rule of thumb, if yours is a small firm with PCs that need checking and which may need upgraded hardware and/or applications, it might cost you anywhere from $150 to $1,500 per PC to achieve compliance. (If you have bought the hardware and/or software recently — within the past two or three years, say — there may be grounds for requiring a no-cost upgrade to make hardware and software compliant.)

Where larger firms have extensive networks or external electronic interfaces that need sorting out, it is almost impossible to fix firmly on a likely cost. Some people in the industry use a very rough rule of thumb of $1,500 per user; but this figure can vary wildly (up and down) depending on complicating factors (e.g., do you use a number of custom applications, is your shopfloor riddled with embedded systems, do you have lots of electronic interfaces with outside bodies?).

Talk to a number of potential consultants to get a feel for the situation, and look around for nearby companies of a similar size and situation; they may give you an idea of what to expect to have to pay. They may also have useful Year 2000 experience to share with you.

## 10.3 Timetables

Keeping your Year 2000 efforts on track will involve doing lots of things at the same time. You will need to set up a series of parallel timetables covering work needed with:

| | |
|---|---|
| **Hardware and software** | Inventory |
| | Analysis |
| | Remedial work |
| | Testing |
| **Automated equipment and embedded systems** | Inventory |
| | Analysis |
| | Remedial work |
| | Testing |
| **Internal data** | Inventory |
| | Analysis |

|  | Documenting and testing |
|  | Setting standards for internal data transfer |
| **Data partners** | Tracking them down |
|  | Agreeing on data transfer methods |
|  | Testing new methods |
| **Suppliers** | Checking for compliance activities |
|  | Assessing eventual compliance |
| **Public utilities** | Checking for compliance activities |
|  | Assessing eventual compliance |
| **Customers** | Checking for compliance activities |
|  | Assessing eventual compliance |

Your timetable should have an escape hatch, in the form of fallback procedures that you can implement should things all go wrong. That "fallback" date we believe should be six months before December 31, 1999, i.e., June 30, 1999. Work all your timetables back from that date.

Setting up a realistic timetable shows that you have considered both the problems that you are already aware of AND the potential problems that might yet emerge. Your timetable may have a certain flexibility built into it — but remember, the final dates are unforgiving and immovable.

## 10.4 Who should do the technical work?

There are two basic possibilities in handling the technical work involved in your Year 2000 project; you can do it yourself, or you can get somebody else to do it. That somebody should be a properly qualified and experienced IT consultant. It is quite possible that within your own organization you have the skills that may be needed to deal with some (if not all) of your Year 2000 problems. The Sources of Help Section contains details of how you can obtain a Technical Pointers Guide if you think you would like to consider coping in-house with your various business applications, operating systems and utilities for Year 2000 compliance.

But remember, if you choose the DIY route, everything you do must be thoroughly documented; and do not let anyone loose on dealing with any aspect of the problem unless you KNOW they know what they are doing. Just taking their word for it could be disastrous — this is no time to be learning on the job.

## 10.5 What is the role of the outside IT consultant?

Where you have decided that your company does not have the right skills and resources to deal with technical matters, or has reached the limits of expertise in these areas, the Year 2000 project manager will need technical assistance provided by a competent, qualified and experienced consultant.

This person needs to be both well-versed in computer technology and (with input from members of your business) have a good understanding of your business. He or she will guide you through the technical work involved in evaluating your computer systems, correcting any Year 2000 problems, and completing testing.

In conjunction with the project manager (who will need to keep control of the purse strings), the consultant will call upon any extra outside personnel and subcontractors needed to carry out any remedial work, always under his or her supervision.

## 10.6 How do I find the right consultant?

There are people out there who see the Year 2000 issue as a means of making a quick buck; they see the opportunity of cashing in even though they do not really have the skills and abilities relevant for the job. There are also a lot of good, well-trained and experienced people in the market who will charge a fair price for doing a solid Year 2000 job for you.

The question is — how do you dodge the former, and track down the latter? None of us wants to be part of someone else's learning curve. The smaller enterprise usually has only limited resources, and will be able to spare the time and money to bring in a consultant once, and once only.

You can narrow down the field by asking prospective consultants a series of questions. We do not pretend that the following is an exhaustive list of possible questions, and you may wish to adapt some of them. But we trust that they will give you some ideas. Send him or her the questions in advance of any interview, and ask for the replies in writing. You can evaluate the answers in your own time, and be ready in the following interview to investigate any areas you think look weak. What you are trying to establish is how much the consultant REALLY KNOWS about the Year 2000 problem and the problems it may cause within a business environment.

**Have you carried out any Year 2000 projects?**
[Ask for a list and references]

**What practical problems arose?**
[Let's make sure the consultants knowledge is based not on theory but real-life practice]

**What non-Year 2000 work have you carried out?**
[Again, ask for references]

**What software tools are you expert in?**
[The consultant needs to understand the software tools that have been used to develop applications in your business]

**Explain the practical relevance of those tools to the applications used by your business**
[Again, this will help to separate theoretical from hands-on knowledge]

**What do you think the implications FOR YOUR FIRM would be of failing to deal effectively with the Year 2000 problem?**
[Let's see if the consultant really understands how the Year 2000 impacts on the smaller enterprise in your sector, if he or she understand the BUSINESS implications]

**What problems do you anticipate in your systems and software?**
[You are looking for detailed and relevant understanding of the issues]

**How do you document projects?**
[You need detailed documentation of all work done]

**How do you report on progress in a project?**
[You will want regular reports on progress]

**Can you describe how you go about testing completed projects?**
[You are looking for signs that testing is taken seriously and carried out methodically — and carefully. You don't want your systems and software tested to destruction! Check the consultant's answers against the suggestions in Section 19]

**How do you propose backing up your systems during work?**
[You need someone who regards backup as essential — and enforces his or her backup routines].

You may find that "consultants" show up bearing new software packages, and insisting that if you buy it as a replacement for your existing software your problems will be solved.

Show them the door. The Year 2000 is a business problem as much as a technical problem; you may be using the software that you use for a specific business purpose. Without knowing both what that purpose is and how your company operates, it is unlikely that anyone could assure you that a new piece of software could safely meet your needs.

At the end of the selection process you will want a guarantee from the consultant that the final result will be fully Year 2000 compliant (see Section 6 on Year 2000 compliance). If the consultant wiggles and shows signs of not wanting to make such guarantees, it's time for the door again.

## 10.7 Doing the inventory
### How big will it be?

In order to find out whether the Year 2000 problem is going to affect your business, you need to know first what computer systems (hardware and software, plus any automated equipment and/or embedded systems) you possess and use; and secondly which ones use dates in such a way as to cause problems come the Year 2000. You will also want to know how data moves between applications and systems and who shares what databases.

For this reason you need to take a complete inventory (physical listing) of all the hardware and software used in your business. It has to be a complete— not a partial — inventory, because only by knowing ALL the facts can you make the right decisions and reduce the potential risks faced by your business.

So, how big is your inventory likely to be? For once, size is everything. For instance, someone who is self-employed and working from home might only have one PC with an office suite of programs (word processing, spreadsheet, database). His or her inventory will be very modest.

Suppose the same person had actually been in business successfully for a few years, and we might find eight or nine people working from rented premises. The business is still categorized as a microfirm, but even a business of this size might find itself building up a hefty inventory — there might be up to 10 PCs of varying ages (and possibly with different operating systems, or different generations of the same system); a small network; and lots of software, probably including an accounting program, word-processing software, a desktop database with a number of applications, spreadsheets with a number of applications ... the inventory may reveal data moving between applications, databases shared by applications, and perhaps data moved externally to and from customers and suppliers as well as payment data made through wire transfers or by credit card terminal.

As the business grows, the networks get more complex. There may be file servers, fax servers, etc. There may be multiple networks in different offices linked together. There may be custom applications (whether written from scratch especially for the company, or package applications that have been specifically modified to meet the company's needs).

In all cases, there may also be remote users with their own PCs, or their own notebooks, laptops, handhelds, etc., all of which may either be used to transmit data into the office or be brought into the office and hooked up to the office network. All these need to be added to the inventory.

And, of course, there is automated equipment with embedded chips in virtually every business, whether only in the fax machine, or in expensive production, retail or distribution equipment.

## Following the data

In addition to checking the systems, you will need to check the way data is passed between systems— both within your own business, and outside to employees and/or subcontractors (e.g., those working from home or from remote offices or working "on the road") and to other organizations.

It is also important to check what data moves between applications. You may find that your database or accounting system may be compliant, but that the spreadsheet from which it takes data is not (or vice versa). You may also find that different versions of the same application transfer date data between each other in a different manner, and so a compliant version of an application may transfer data to and from a noncompliant version of the same application, and so end up corrupted too.

All this work may seem excessive, but it will bring benefits if the information arising from your inventory is used intelligently. You may find out a lot more about the way your company operates than you knew before you started doing the inventory. Indeed, one of the positive aspects of Year 2000 activity is that it puts your entire business under the spotlight and forces you to think — hard — about what you're doing and the way you're doing it.

Most of us do not make the time for such a close scrutiny under normal circumstances. You may as a result be able to streamline the way you do business and improve the way the company operates based on the new knowledge you have acquired.

### Taking the inventory

You need to draw up inventory forms (Sources of Help, tells you how to obtain samples) that you can use to take stock of your:

■ Hardware;
■ Software (including interfaces to other systems); and
■ Embedded systems.

You will need to fill out one form for EACH piece of software (including operating system, utilities, interface software between applications and applications), EACH piece of hardware, and EACH piece of automated equipment that might be affected by embedded systems. As you can only make decisions about your systems when you have full information in hand, all points on the forms should be completed. Don't leave any blanks; if you don't have the right information available as you complete the form, write "NOT APPLICABLE" or "NOT KNOWN." Later you will need to review all the completed forms for these statements.

All the forms you use need to contain the following:

■ The name of the person (and his or her supervisor) who dealt with the inventory of each item;
■ A unique reference number;
■ The identifying information and description of the item, including version and/or model number;
■ Its user(s); and

■ The HOW, WHAT and WHY of its use.

There is more information that you will need to log depending on what you are investigating.

### Software

- On what system(s) are the programs and data for this software held;
- What data is created on it;
- Who shares that data (both internally and externally);
- What databases are shared;
- With what other applications;
- Are there plans for this data and these databases to be shared with other parties;
- Are there new applications being developed that would link to this data or these databases;
- How is past data archived;
- Who supplied the software;
- Do you know the supplier's present whereabouts;
- What language was used to develop the software (for custom software only — see Sections 10.10 and 13);
- Where is the source code, documentation and specification (custom);
- Has anyone modified the software since it was originally written (custom), and if so how;
- Are there any amendments/modifications planned or in progress;
- Who maintains the software and/or provides updates;
- What was a) the original cost b) the costs of any modifications/ amendments;
- Any ongoing costs (maintenance, upgrading, debugging etc.);
- The expected life of the software;
- Are there any known Year 2000 problems;
- Who is available to fix any Year 2000 problems;
- Is the software Year 2000 compliant, based on the author's statements;
- If changes are needed, what will the cost be;
- What are the alternatives, including cost;
- Where are the license/warranty/maintenance agreements; and

- Are there any hidden "nasties" in the way the product is licensed (including the possibility that testing for date changes may destroy programs and data)?

## Hardware

- Who supplied the hardware;
- What software runs on the hardware;
- Has the hardware been checked for compliance;
- Who maintains it, and has it been checked for Year 2000 compliance;
- What was a) the original cost b) the cost of upgrades and additions since then;
- The ongoing costs of maintenance and support (identify suppliers of these services);
- Are there any plans to 1) add to or 2) replace the hardware;
- If changes are needed, what will the cost be;
- What are the alternatives, including cost?

## Automated equipment/embedded systems

- Who supplied the equipment, and is the company still in business;
- Who is the manufacturer, and is the company still in business;
- Who installed and tested the equipment, and is the company still in business;
- Who, if anybody, did any programming, and is the company still in business;
- Who maintains the equipment, and has the company been checked for Year 2000 compliance;
- Has the manufacturer confirmed that the equipment is compliant;
- Has it been tested for compliance;
- Does it process date-related data for use only by itself;
- Does it receive date-related data from (or pass it to) other equipment or computer systems;
- What was 1) the original cost, 2) the cost of upgrades and additions since the original purchase;

- The ongoing costs of maintenance and support (identify suppliers of these services);
- Are there plans to a) add to or b) replace the equipment;
- If changes are needed, what will it cost;
- What are the alternatives, including cost.?

In smaller firms, the owner/manager should probably take the inventory. In larger firms, either set up an inventory team to work its way through the whole business, or ask departmental managers to take inventories of their own areas. Note that if you do the latter, you should reinforce the process with spot checks.

In all cases, you will be looking especially to see whether your applications, and the links sending data between applications, are using two-digit or four-digit years. If the application uses two-digit years, you may find that it uses a "window" to allow it to recognize dates beyond 2000 (see Section 10.13 for details). If so, you will need to log what kind of windowing technique has been used. You will also need to investigate the kind of data that is archived within the application, and the archived documents themselves. If this data is important but cannot be brought into a four-digit environment, you will need to find a way of preserving it (see Section 10.9).

## Linking the systems together with uses and users

When the inventory is completed, you will need to create a database to store all this information. You should use the information to create a total picture of how all your systems fit together. You will almost certainly find this easiest if you draw up some flow charts; these will help make clear which systems really drive the business, and so which are the most important to fix.

In a very small business this may be very obvious, but as the business gets bigger (and more systems or softwares are used) it becomes less easy to see without this kind of analysis of the level of dependence of the business on any specific piece of technology.

## Guidance for larger firms

In a business with different departments run by different managers, you will inevitably find that managers' views of their own departments may not be identical with yours. They may, for example, have spent a lot of money investing in a piece of software, and feel that they must boost its importance or lose face. However, the objective truth may be that this cherished piece of software is too-elaborate for the task it is being asked to carry out, or is underpinning an operation that is peripheral to the core business. It is only by drawing up a detailed overview that you can rise above these partisan interests and take a broad overview of the business as a whole.

## 10.8 Prioritize all applications

The information gathered during the inventory, plus the chart showing how everything fits together, will allow you to draw up a clear list of all the systems in the business in order of priority, with the "mission-critical" ones firmly at the top.

We emphasize: MISSION-CRITICAL FIRST.

It would be crazy to spend your time dealing with the systems that can be fixed easily (but which are not vital to the business) only to find that your firm collapsed because you hadn't focused your company's attention on the systems that really mattered to its survival.

It may help clarify your thinking if you place your applications into one of four lists:

- Mission-critical systems;
- Very important systems;
- Less important systems; and
- Unimportant systems.

**Mission-critical systems** are those core applications that run the business as a whole. Without them, the business might come to a grinding halt and possibly collapse. These, typically, might include applications controlling invoicing, the sales ledger, stock control, and the production and distribution systems.

**Very important systems** are those that may drive a part of the business. The failure of these would cause severe disruption (but not, in all probability, the failure of the business), and might cause the company to be less competitive and less efficient. These, for example, might include sales and marketing systems.

**Less important systems** are ones whose failure might cause inconvenience internally (and possibly some impact on internal efficiency), but would not affect the company in regard to the outside world. There will usually be a way of transferring the tasks to manual/paper operation, or creating some other kind of work-around method. These might include such things as payroll systems or human resources applications.

**Unimportant systems** are those whose failure would have no impact on the business whatsoever. A database of magazines or books, for example, might fall into this category.

Other areas of "mission criticality" relate to archived data and business records, as the next section describes.

## 10.9 Check how you deal with archived data and documents

Technology changes constantly, but data is here forever. Your business may have stacks and stacks of data that was logged using a system that is no longer in use. Sorting out the Year 2000 problem may seem like a good opportunity to clean out the files— but beware, some of this data might include documents that need to be retained to keep the legal, tax or regulatory authorities happy.

The real killer is that often there is a requirement that this data be preserved in its original form— which would prohibit changing the date fields from two to four digits! You will need to establish whether the software tools that you use to read archived data will still function after December 31, 1999. You will also need to ensure that you can safeguard the right versions of the programs that you have been using to update and process archived data.

If you are able in this way to ensure that you always have access to the archived data in its original form (perhaps through a solitary, stand-alone machine somewhere in the business), you might then be able to make a full copy, and then make the copied version Year 2000 compliant (by date change, windowing, etc.) so that you can access it throughout the business to meet day-to-day needs. Should you ever need the originals in their original, noncompliant state, you will still have access to them.

Ultimately, if you think that losing access to your archived documents could become a mission-critical issue (e.g., a regulator might close you down if you can't produce the right information), there is one simple, if laborious, option; print everything out, create a filing system, and store the documents with backup copies off-site.

## 10.10 Different kinds of applications will need different tactics

As different resources, skills and actions may be needed for different types of applications, break them down into different categories. The way you would deal with a software package which is covered by a maintenance contract is very different from the way you would handle a program which was written specially for you years ago, but whose author has long since vanished.

### Package applications

These are programs that have been sold as packages by a commercial software company in a standard format with standard documentation. Users may have some ability to configure them for their own tastes. Often, firms will have maintenance agreements covering these packages as well as some degree of support from the manufacturers.

## Custom applications

These are programs that have been written specifically for your business, either by a commercial software company, or by consultants, or by your own people. The term "custom application" also covers packages which have been substantially modified or tailored for your own company's use. There will also be applications developed from commercial databases and spreadsheets, some of which may well be part of mission-critical operations, providing important reports or tracking valuable company information.

## Internal interfaces

Data moved between people, systems and applications within the firm.

## External interfaces

Data moved between the company and other organizations, e.g., banks or your suppliers and customers. These organizations are your "data partners."

## Hardware

## Operating system software and utilities

## Automated equipment and embedded systems

## 10.11 The big decision: repair, replace, or scrap?

The steps you have taken up until now will have presented you with all the information you need to move on to the big decision — what to do with your various systems, if they are found to have Year 2000 problems. You will know which these are, because either your own tests will reveal problems, or the software authors or suppliers and the hardware manufacturers may confirm that there are problems, or your consultants may uncover problems.

You must now, broadly speaking, decide which of three tactics to adopt for each system or application:

REPAIR IT;
REPLACE IT; or
SCRAP IT.

### Repair (modify/upgrade)

If the system is important to you and carrying out modifications or an upgrade is simple and straightforward, this is the route you should probably choose. This presupposes that you have access to the author/publisher/manufacturer of the software, and that they are able to provide you with the necessary Year 2000 compliant upgrades. If you have let your maintenance or support contracts lapse, you should expect to have to pay some or all of your back charges.

If there are no upgrades available, you will have to convert the dates.

### Replace

You may decide that, for one or more of your existing systems or software applications, it would be better to replace the whole thing, and that this will be a better alternative (more reliable, less costly, more desirable features, etc.) to modification. It may well be that you had thought about replacing it some time ago, and that the arrival of the Year 2000 issue simply gives you the opportunity to go ahead.

Where a manufacturer states that it is not certain whether their product is compliant, or that it no longer supports the product, or you get the feeling that the company neither knows nor cares, it is probably wisest to change the product and find another supplier. (If you bought the product expecting it to work beyond January 1, 2000, you may have a legal right of action on the basis that the product is not fit for the purpose for which you purchased it, or that it has caused you damage — the costs of replacement/repair, loss of profits, etc. Check with your legal advisers.)

Some companies are moving in the direction of buying a new system (costs are capitalized) rather than modifying the existing one (costs are written off against current profits), because they believe that this will show their published accounts in a better light. This is a dangerous way to do business, since the balance sheet improvements (if any) will probably be far outweighed by the damage to the business if the new system doesn't function properly. The bottom line is survival — not accounting cleverness.

BEWARE! Because time is of the essence with Year 2000 problems, you MUST be sure that the replacement system will be in place, fully functional and available for testing and training by the beginning of 1999 AT THE LATEST. If you have any doubts, steer clear of this solution. Remember that most IT projects have a nasty habit of busting their timetables — but the Year 2000 is one deadline that cannot be pushed back.

### Scrap

If you decide that you no longer need a system or piece of software, probably because it no longer meets the needs of the business, then you might decide to scrap it. There may be systems that are no longer used, or software that was bought for a purpose but was never used and the purpose no longer exists. You may wish to use this opportunity to clean up your systems. You may find that you can make substantial savings in hardware and software costs, maintenance and support, by getting rid of the dead wood.

If you do scrap systems or software, check that you are not disposing of data which IS valuable to the business. This data should be capable of transfer to another system if in a common format such as Text (.txt), dBase (.dbf), etc.

## 10.12 Working through the project with the consultant

If you decide to employ an outside IT consultant, he or she will need to work very closely with the Year 2000 project manager, and will need to go through the following involved steps:

(1) Set out a detailed plan of technical work to be done, carefully diagrammed for ease of explanation and presentation, and with a project management system so that nothing gets missed. This plan may, of course, change as circumstances arise, but it must be monitored on a regular basis, and the Year 2000 project manager should regularly report on progress. Some key decision dates will need to be set down, and these should be met if the project is to finish on time.

(2) Take the information from the inventory of systems and, where the original author is not going to do the rectification work for you, examine the program code, system by system, to identify date fields and the use of dates within other fields (such as indexes). The consultant then needs to establish what effect these date occurrences have on the application by following these through programs and system data, and examine the impact on input screens and printed reports and queries.

(3) Estimate the time and resources needed to modify the code to eliminate any Year 2000 problems. The consultant will also be expected to define the skills required by other personnel involved in the project, and to assign them their work. He or she will also set down a timetable of work (integrated with the detailed plan in (1) above), and set down dates for progress review. Keeping to the dates is vital.

(4) Arrange for the remedial work to be carried out under continuous and close supervision.

(5) Establish a strict regime that ensures that applications, programs and systems that have been made compliant do not interact with applications, programs and systems that are still noncompliant. If this regime is not observed, then data could be sent from compliant system A to noncompliant application B, which changes the data and sends it back corrupted to A, which in turn passes it on to system C etc. Compliant system A would thus end up producing noncompliant data.

(6) Complete all testing before bringing the newly-compliant applications, programs and systems into the live business environment. See Section 19 for more details.

## 10.13 Converting two-digit dates

If whatever system or application you are working on cannot be upgraded or modified by the original author or manufacturer, but you do not wish to replace it or scrap it, then you will have to modify it by moving it from a two-digit date environment to a four-digit one. (This presupposes that you have access to at least the program source code for the application, and have the skills and resources to carry out the work.)

The ideal way of correcting any two-digit dates (e.g., "97") found in systems or applications is physically to rewrite them, changing them into four-digit dates (e.g., "1997"). This is known as "date expansion." The advantage of this method is that, if properly carried out, it will deliver full Year 2000 compliance for the system or application concerned. The disadvantage is that it takes time (and can therefore also be expensive, in that it chews up man-hours). Our general view is that the saying "four digits good, two digits bad" is a sensible one, and we recommend this approach if you can be sure of completing the work in good time.

There is another technique called "windowing," whereby the two-digit dates are left written as two digits, but the program or system is set up so that when it encounters a two-digit date it *assumes* the century. A typical windowing solution might assume that any year date between 00 and 29 would be a 21st century date, so that "13" would be assumed to mean 2013. All other numbers from 30 to 99 would be assumed to be 20th century, so that "49" would be assumed to be 1949.

The advantage of this method is that it is quicker than date expansion. The disadvantage is that it can give rise to problems if data is transferred between systems or applications that use different windows. The other main disadvantage is that occasionally you might encounter a date where the wrong century will be assumed (with the window described above, if a birth date of February 20, 1929, was encountered — 02/20/29 — the system would assume, wrongly, that the 29 meant 2029). For these reasons, we suggest you look at other solutions before turning to windowing.

However, if you are running out of time, clearly windowing remains an option, provided that you are aware of its disadvantages and take steps to counter likely problems. These steps include making detailed documentation of the way you define and handle the windows so that future users know what solution has been used, and how it has been implemented, if they need to modify or replace the application.

# 11. What can go wrong with hardware and software — and when?

## 11.1 Different kinds of non-compliance

With the Year 2000, as with so much in life, things are not simply black and white. You will find, if you have problems, that some are worse than others — or just different. The following list, while not exhaustive, covers most of the things that can go wrong with hardware and software in the Year 2000:

- Some programs will not work at all after December 31, 1999;
- Some programs that seem to recognize January 1, 2000 do not recognize that 2000 is a Leap Year;
- Some programs that seem to recognize 2000 as a Leap Year may not recognize that it has 366 days;
- Some programs can be modified to work after December 31, 1999, but, after that modification, fail to work correctly before that date (i.e., right now);
- Some programs only permit the input of the year with two digits (not four), and assume the century. If you cannot get into the main operating system to change the century from the 20th to the 21st, then after December 31, 1999, the program will most likely assume that it is January 1, 1900, resulting in a loss and/or corruption of data, or possibly a system failure; and
- Where programs handle dates in different date formats (i.e., some work only in the 20th century, while others work correctly in the

21st century), data can be incorrectly transferred between applications, resulting in the loss and/or corruption of data, or possibly system failure.

Where a manufacturer claims compliance for software, you need to be sure that it will not fall into *any* of the categories above. That means that you need to know what kind of tests have been carried out.

For example, people who have carried out the by now infamous "rollover" test on their PCs (simply setting the date to just before midnight on December 31, 1999, and then waiting to see what happens). DO NOT TRY THIS YOURSELF unless you really know what you are doing, (see Section 16.1). You may assume that because January 1, 2000 showed up that all is well. But for all they know, the machine will turn up its toes later in 2000 because it does not recognize the Leap Year — it *seems* compliant, but actually is nothing of the sort.

In the same way, you need to confirm that the manufacturer has checked that the software he is claiming is compliant has been checked while running on a system similar to yours. You need to be sure that the software will work in combination with *your* version of PC running on *your* version of the operating system. This goes internally, too; if you run two or more versions of an operating system across your various machines, you cannot assume that because the software tested OK on machines using the newer system, that it will work just as well when applied to machines running the older version.

## 11.2  When will things start to go wrong?

If an application or piece of hardware is going to fail, then the date of that failure is called its "event horizon." You should be aware that many event horizons will fall *before* January 1, 2000 — and in these cases, clearly you have less time available to fix them than you think. Early failure will often occur where a system is required to look at dates in the future, and compare them to another date, often today's date. Some of these systems, when asked to look at a date beyond 1999, see what they think is an invalid date, and therefore crash or malfunction. This was found, for instance, on credit card systems where credit cards with expiration dates in the year 2000 were being rejected by some credit card terminals in 1997.

In other cases, event horizons may be dictated by the way the authors of the software constructed their programs or applications. Sometimes these early event horizons are caused by programmers picking dates (which seemed way in the future when they wrote the programs) which they used for fixed maintenance schedules, such as deleting archived data. They include:

- January 1, 1999 (1/1/99);
- September 9, 1999 (9/9/99); and
- December 31, 1999 (12/31/99).

There may be others that we are not yet aware of. So it is always worth looking in the documentation and system setup files for dates with special meanings that might end up dictating the event horizon.

## 11.3 Illegal software

Your inventory of systems and software may uncover illegal software— either pirated material or programs and applications that have been placed on PC hard disks without having been bought by your organization, or legitimate applications which have just been copied beyond the terms of their original license.

It is important that you either stop the use of illegal software you uncover, or regulate matters by paying the appropriate license fee. If you continue to use the software without doing that, and the use of that software has become important to your business, you are likely to find your business in great difficulty.

If the authorities discover the illegal software, the very fact that you have carried out an inventory will rob you of the defense of ignorance (which is in any case not much of a defense).

## 11.4 Shareware

Many businesses use shareware which has either been copied by one of the firm's users around the building or has been downloaded from the Internet. This shareware often consists of nifty little utilities — but some shareware programs may actually have become essential to the day-to-day running of your business.

It is important to register for a Year 2000 compliant version, if such exists. If none exists, find another utility and get rid of the shareware program.

# 12. Dealing with package applications

## 12.1 So many applications, so little compliance

In the spring of 1997, a well-known computer consulting firm completed Year 2000 testing on 4,000 off-the-shelf PC software packages — and two-thirds of them ran in ways that were noncompliant. Spreadsheet, database, accounting and payroll applications in particular were found to have problems. Just because the application has a well-known name on the side of the box does not mean that the contents are safe. You have to satisfy yourself that they will be Year 2000 compliant.

## 12.2 First actions

The first thing to do with a package application is to contact the software company that provides your software support to find out whether the version of the application you are looking at is Year 2000 compliant. If not, find out what you have to do to run a compliant version in-house. If you do not have a company supporting you, you will have to go straight to the manufacturer of the package. In either case, ask what tests they have carried out to check for Year 2000 compliance. These should include all the tests that we list in the section on testing (Section 19).

Where there is no compliant version, and there is no likelihood of a compliant version becoming available within a reasonable time, then you will need to replace it with other package software which is suitable to your needs — and which is Year 2000 compliant. Where the package manufacturer has gone out of business (and there is no software company supporting the product with a Year 2000 compliant version), you should follow the same procedure as if there was no compliant version.

## 12.3 Leave plenty of time to set up a replacement

Working backwards from December 1999, you should allow a year for installation, training, testing and running the new package in parallel with your existing system. That means that *before the end of 1998* you will need to:

■ Analyze how the existing software fits into your business, how you use it and what it does for you. (You may also want to create a "wish-list" of additional features that you would ideally like when searching for a new off-the-shelf package.) Don't forget that the staff who use the programs will have a lot of valuable and practical input;

■ Select an alternative software package that fits your needs, and which is Year 2000 compliant, and whose manufacturer is able to warrant unreservedly that it is Year 2000 compliant, and is able to provide you with information about the tests they have run to check this; and

■ Satisfy yourself that the supplier has adequate resources (or can recommend competent computer consultants) to help you install and test the software, and to train your staff in its use.

We consider that it may take you some time to complete the process described in the three points above.

# 13. Dealing with custom applications

From your inventory, you may have identified some custom applications, i.e., those written specifically for your company by a commercial software company, or by consultants, or by your own employees. Such applications could also include one or more package applications which have been substantially modified for your company's own needs.

Where the application has been written by in-house personnel using desktop databases and spreadsheets, please see Section 14 "Dealing with desktop-developed applications."

You will want to find out from the author of the software whether the product is Year 2000 compliant, and if so, what checks and tests he or she has carried out to confirm this. Those tests should give you the kind of results you could expect from the tests shown in Section 19. If you cannot trace the author, either because he or she has left the area or gone out of business, or because the author is an ex-employee who has moved on, then you will have to test the software yourself.

If it is not Year 2000 compliant, you will need to find out whether it can be modified for compliance, and, if so, when. If the author cannot commit to complete the required work in good time (i.e., so that all testing and retraining required can be completed before the end of 1998), you should start looking for an alternative.

Who should bear the cost of this work? That depends on the circumstances, such as when the application was written (the longer ago, the more likely it is that you will have to pay), who wrote it (if it was an employee, clearly you will have to pay), and the terms of the contract under which it was supplied, including any warranties, guarantees, etc. But you need to get the application fixed *right now*, not end up in a legal battle — so if there is a dispute over payment it is probably best to ask your lawyer for advice on how to get the work done without giving up any legal rights you may have.

If you either cannot find the original author or cannot get him or her to agree to terms for doing the work, or he or she cannot spare you the time to do it, there are a number of alternatives you could consider:

- If the author is available for supervision, you could find someone else who is competent to carry out the modifications or conversion to make the application Year 2000 compliant working with or under the guidance of the author;
- If the author is not available, you could find someone else who is competent to carry out the modifications or conversion to make the application Year 2000 compliant working without any assistance from the original author. This person would need access to the original application/program specification, documented programs (computer print-out) and source code (documented programs on disk or tape). There may be copyright issues here, although if you are taking action to enable the software to work correctly on the equipment for which it was purchased, the copyright holder might not be able to contest your action. Check with your legal adviser;
- You could opt to buy a packaged application that does the job currently being done by the custom application. For instance, you may have had a custom accounting, invoice and order processing system written for you some time ago. Today, there are lots of all-in-one package programs on the market that can do this job, but you would need to check that they do not leave out any functions that are vital to your needs; or

■ You could ask someone to write a new custom application. Because time is running out, this may be dangerous, unless you can find someone who uses Rapid Applications Development tools and methodologies, and is able to commit 100% of his or her time to dealing with your application. You MUST have the application in place by December 1998 for testing and training, etc. — there is no room for slippage!

# 14. Dealing with desktop-developed applications

When carrying out the inventory of software, you may find applications that have been written using developments of popular spreadsheets and databases. These may have been written by your staff (past or present), or by outside consultants or software companies acting on your behalf.

Such spreadsheets and databases may handle two-digit dates in different ways, and this may be the case even within different versions of the same manufacturer's products. (For instance, different versions of the popular Microsoft applications Access and Excel do not handle two-digit dates in the same way.)

This can cause problems when data is moved between the applications, and you may find that if you send data containing a year date like 2005 from one desktop application to another, the second will interpret it as 1905. The only answer is to look for and eliminate all applications using two-digit dates, either by repairing them or replacing them with four-digit versions. Do not assume that because you find one version of a desktop application is compliant, that all the other versions of the same application are also compliant. Test them all, and the links between them, using the procedures described in Section 19.

Please note that if you have been using two-digit years and rewrite them to four-digit years, certain other changes will need to be made, including reformatting screens and printed reports, as well as possible changes to program logic and macros. When dealing with these desktop applications, use the procedures for dealing with custom applications described in the previous section. Further information on two-digit years in connection with popular databases and spreadsheets is contained in the Technical Pointers Guide of the Year 2000 Survival Pack — see the Sources of Help section.

# 15. Dealing with interface and data partners

## 15.1 Transmitting data internally between applications and systems

It is vital to ensure that data flowing around inside your business, from application to application or between different computer systems, is not corrupted by incorrect date information. So it is essential when you are checking and testing your internal systems to make sure that all year date information included in data transmitted between applications or systems is transmitted consistently in the correct four-digit date format. Sometimes the method of transmission itself — the interface — can be non-compliant. You can render a system and all its applications compliant, and still find that when it takes the compliant data and transmits it, the data arrives in a noncompliant state. So you must test all the internal links as well as the applications, programs and systems themselves.

DON'T FORGET that this transfer of data can happen not just using electronic links, but using floppy disks, data storage devices, tape, etc. Your inventory should reveal all these links and methods of transferring data between applications; be suspicious of all of them.

## 15.2 Transmitting data externally to and from data partners

More and more businesses transmit data between each other. Whether this is between a business and its bank, or between a business and its customers and suppliers, or between a business and its subsidiaries or partners (think of a network of car dealerships, for example) the principles are the same. One company creates data in its system; that data is sent via an electronic (software) bridge or gateway; and it is received and interpreted by the recipient so that it can be used in the recipient's computer system.

The most visible forms of data transfer are credit card terminals in stores and cash machines in banks, where you can use one bank's cash machine to draw money from your account at another bank.

There is little point in going to a lot of effort to get your own business Year 2000 compliant if you are busily receiving noncompliant data from an outside organization. These electronic links are full of potential problems — date information may be used and held differently in the software application run by the sender, in the software application run by the recipient, and in the software application used by the bridge or gateway.

Part of your inventory process will involve finding out who your external data partners are. You should log all data exchanges, including data transmitted over telephone lines and data transferred by computer media, such as floppy disks, tapes, Zip, Jaz, SyQuest, etc. You might transmit data over the telephone or ISDN lines to your bank, or to a customer or supplier. You might also send a floppy disk with data to be processed (e.g., a mailing list) to an external company. What happens if that company's systems cannot process it for some reason? All these transfer systems will have to be checked for compliance.

This will mean cooperating with your data partners, and agreeing to establish compatible methods, formats and content of data exchanges. It may also mean that until you can both get a compatible and compliant system of exchanging data up and running, tested and installed, that you may have to suspend temporarily transfers of data or find another way of getting the information across.

# 16. Dealing with hardware, operating system software and utilities

## 16.1 Checking and fixing hardware

It is essential to ensure that all hardware the business relies on to run its operations will handle dates accurately both before, during and after January 1, 2000.

In the case of your computer systems, the first line of approach is usually to go back to the original supplier or to the company that provides you with maintenance support. In the case of PCs, you can check your desktop machines and servers for compliance either manually or by using one of the commercially-available software programs that examine your BIOS (Basic Input/Output System) or RTC (Real Time Clock). There are other programs that will not only carry out these checks, but will also attempt to fix any Year 2000 problems. Some of these programs are better than others.

In essence, these testing tools (or the manual tests that you can carry out) check to see whether the PC will be able to make the transition from December 31, 1999 to January 1, 2000, in one piece, both powered-on and powered-off, and whether it will recognize that 2000 is a Leap Year.

If it fails, all is not lost; further tests might show whether the transition can be managed by a software fix (which stays resident in the PC's memory until 2000), or whether you can carry out a manual fix. The latter may involve you remembering to power off your machine in 1999, and running the fix as soon as you restart in 2000. This is manageable if you are computer-aware and running just one or two machines — but if you are running a number of machines, this could turn into quite a daunting task, and a software fix might be a better bet. (Even if you are running a PC network where all the machines take their date from the network server, you must still check ALL the machines, so that if they ever run as stand-alones — when the network goes down, for example — they don't cause problems or corrupt any data.)

If tests show that a fix isn't possible, you may have to go back to the manufacturer to get an amended BIOS. If that isn't available, then you will have to replace the PC with a new model, but make certain that it is GUARANTEED IN WRITING to be Year 2000 compliant — and test it as soon as you get it out of its wrapping, just in case.

WARNING! All checks of the BIOS and RTC should be done by a competent computer engineer, or someone in your business who KNOWS what they are doing. All systems should be completely backed up before any checks are carried out. This is vital, because if your system fails the test, you could lose data and find that some of your computer programs no longer work. Even if it passes, you may find that some time-limited software will stop working.

## 16.2 Operating system software

Unless you already wanted to upgrade your operating system, and will therefore take the opportunity presented by the Year 2000 issue to do so, you may find that it will be more cost-effective to get a patch or fix from the manufacturer without upgrading— which will frequently involve you having to spend lots of cash on new memory and hard disks, plus training costs, plus additional support costs, etc.

In any case, you will need to set the operating system so that the date format contains four-digit years by adding the two extra digits for the century (i.e., 19 or 20). This simple step can help with some of the potential problems in many applications, which often look to the operating system's date format as a guide to how they should handle dates.

## 16.3 Back-up software

There's little point in fixing your systems if the back-up system and software you use is not Year 2000 compliant. Check this carefully, and don't forget to check the PC on which you run the back-up system!

If you send your data off-site electronically, you should treat the storage company as a data partner (see Section 15.2). If you take back-ups on disks or tapes off-site, make sure that any machine (a PC at home, for example) that might be used to read the backed-up data is also checked for Year 2000 compliance.

## 16.4 Anti-virus software

In many systems, the first piece of software to run when the system is booted up is the virus checker. This tends to compare the system date and the dates on the files. If the system date is before all the file dates contained on the computer (because the computer has Year 2000 problems and thinks it's either 1900 or 1980), it will not recognize the files, and some viruses may slip into your system.

This is another reason (as if there weren't enough already!) to ensure that ALL your PCs and servers are checked for Year 2000 compliance.

## 16.5 Maintenance and replacement machines

A simple point, but one which can be missed: some businesses keep replacement PCs and other hardware as back-up machines, or use them when other machines are being maintained. Other businesses have third-party maintenance companies that hold stocks of machines for replacement purposes. All these must be checked for compliance too.

It is easy to forget that even the most ancient, creaking PC kept locked in a dark cupboard should be rendered compliant or escorted to the nearest dump if it's beyond repair — or one day, somebody whose machine has broken down will drag it out, dust it down, and plug it in ...

## 16.6 Facilities management and outsourced systems

Many businesses have some of their computer information processed by outsiders. These could include a computer bureau (e.g., handling your payroll, sales ledger or mailing lists) or a facilities manager looking after the entire running of the computer department.

In all cases it is vital for you to check that these outsiders are going to be able to provide you with an uninterrupted service after December 31, 1999. There are stories of facilities managers who have stated that so awful are the problems in the systems that they are running that they plan to throw in the towel during 1999 and leave their clients in the lurch.

Get your legal adviser to check over all the contracts you have with these outsiders as a matter of urgency; if there is even a technical possibility that they could terminate the agreement with you, start action now to find an alternative solution, and put a risk management plan in place without delay.

# 17. Network issues

In dealing with networks and other multiuser systems, the following are some of the Year 2000 issues to consider:

- Has an **inventory** been made of all the tools, utilities and applications on the network?
- Is the **server hardware** compliant?
- Are **operating systems** compliant?
- Are all network **connections** (bridges, routers, hubs, etc.) compliant?
- Is all network **management software** compliant?
- Are all **compilers and development tools** compliant? Are changes needed to existing applications?
- Are all **applications** (package, custom and desktop) compliant?
- Are **utilities** (back-up? antivirus? others?) compliant?
- Are all **peripheral servers** compliant?
- Are all **workstations** checked for compliance?
- Have all systems that are (or may be) **attached** to the network been checked for compliance? (This includes notebooks, laptops, handhelds, palmtops, including any owned by employees which they might one day bring to work and plug in, or connect to the network remotely over telephone lines. All these devices may handle dates differently.)
- Have you checked all the machines held by you or a third party company for **maintenance or replacement or back-up**?

■ Has a procedure been established for setting standards for dates **transferred**?

- Between applications on the network?
- Between different networks within the organization?
- Between the organization and external bodies?
- Have **gateways** been established to handle noncompliant dates in transmitted data?

# 18. Dealing with automated equipment and embedded systems

In Section 4.7, we gave an outline of the problems that might occur with embedded and automated systems, and there is more relevant information contained in Appendix Six.

In practice, most of the steps you can take in dealing with these systems mirror actions you would take for other systems:

- Take an inventory of all automated equipment and embedded systems;
- Establish their criticality to your business;
- Check where date-data is received from, or transferred to, other automated equipment or computer systems;
- If the equipment was built in your premises by your own engineers, use your skilled engineers to test the equipment offline. If your engineers don't have the right skills, subcontract some who do. Ensure that all tests are fully documented. There may be safety considerations involved. If the problem cannot be fixed, you will need to make a decision to replace or scrap the systems;
- If the equipment was bought in, contact the manufacturers. If they confirm — in writing — that it is Year 2000 compliant ask for details of the tests they carried out to check compliance. Note that two machines of the same make and model, even if they appear identical, can have the same chip programmed differently, or different chips

— making one machine compliant and one machine noncompliant. There's no way to be sure without testing them all;

■ Where there is a problem with Year 2000 compliance, the manufacturer may replace or reprogram the relevant chips. If this is not possible, you may need to replace the machine. Who bears the cost will depend on the circumstances — but your main consideration must be to have a machine (the repaired original or a replacement) ready for the Year 2000 in plenty of time. Your legal adviser should be able to give you advice on how to preserve your legal position while you get on with the job of getting the machine ready;

■ Prepare contingency plans in case you fail to get your equipment Year 2000 compliant in time.

# 19. Testing — the key to success

## 19.1 The importance of testing cannot be overstated

It is imperative that you ensure that the systems and software you think (or have been told) are Year 2000 compliant actually ARE compliant, and that you ensure that systems and software that have been converted or modified to be Year 2000 compliant ARE compliant, and REMAIN compliant. Compliance means 100% compliance of all systems on which the survival, competitiveness and efficiency of the business depend. This can be established beyond doubt only by testing.

Once you have prioritized your systems, testing is the most important aspect of work needed to check their Year 2000 compliance status or to make them Year 2000 compliant. You may find testing takes as much as 60% to 70% of your Year 2000 effort, both in terms of time and cash — this is the reason you need to start the total effort NOW.

Testing can be long and tedious— but it is vital to your operation and should not be the subject of shortcuts. If your testing is incomplete, you may find out the hard way that you or your consultant have correctly fixed 99% of date problems in the program code, but allowed 1% to escape. That 1% could cause data corruption and chaos after December 31, 1999.

You can test individual pieces of equipment or software for Year 2000 compliance until you're blue in the face, and still end up with a non-compliant system.

Why? Because none of these programs, applications and bits of hardware work in isolation; they all form part of a system (or systems) that interact with other programs, applications and bits of hardware, located both within your own business and externally. You need the help and input of the users themselves, as it is they who generally know what their systems should do and how they work together.

Testing needs to be well-planned and methodically carried out. It requires full written details to be taken— scripts of the tests to be carried out and methods used (these will vary between different applications and systems), the results of those tests, any comments on and/or evaluation of those results, and full information about the person(s) who carried out the tests and their supervisor (if any).

Any errors discovered from the tests will need to be retested after they are corrected, and the process repeated until no further errors occur. These tests must cover:

- ALL hardware;
- ALL operating systems;
- ALL key utilities (back-up, antivirus, access control, etc.);
- ALL software development tools;
- ALL applications software;
- ALL desktop applications, including all components of office suites;
- ALL databases;
- ALL movements of data between
  - (a) systems
  - (b) applications on the same system (e.g., between spreadsheets, or between spreadsheets and databases)
  - (c) the company and its remote users (staff, subcontractors, etc.) across Wide Area Networks (WANs), etc.
  - (d) the company and its data partners;

- ALL automated equipment/embedded systems; and
- ALL interfaces between automated equipment and
  - (a) other equipment in your organization
  - (b) other computers in your organization
  - (c) computers in other organizations.

We have used the term ALL above. This may seem unreasonable if you propose to scrap a system late in 1999. However, that system may process transactions which cover the period from now to 2000 (e.g., a 12- or 24-month contract) and may not be able to handle them.

Furthermore, a system may produce data which may be entered into other systems which you HAVE tested for compliance. Unless you can isolate that system so that no data is transferred in or out of it, it must be included in your testing. When each of the items of hardware, together with each of the items of software on them, have been tested and have passed all their tests, then it will be necessary to test all the databases and data movements in careful and controlled order to check that they contain only compliant data, and that they process only compliant data.

This will require that you have a very detailed roadmap of your data movements (collected from the inventory) and that you check every route of data movement.

### 19.2 The five test conditions your software and systems need to pass

The Technical Pointers Guide contained in our Year 2000 Survival Pack carries detailed information governing the principles of testing, and some tips and tricks you can use. But in general, ALL systems and software should be tested to establish that:

- They can continue to work in the period up to and including December 31, 1999. You don't want your business applications to be modified and put back into regular use in 1999 only to discover that they might well work correctly in 2000, but do not now work in 1999;

■ They can, without problem, process transactions up to December 31, 1999, that affect transactions after that date, e.g., a contract for regular orders or payments with expiration date after December 31, 1999;

■ They can process transactions and reports over the period December 1, 1999 to February 1, 2000, correctly and without problems. The purpose of this test is to find out if they handle the month ends for December 1999 and January 2000 without any problems;

■ They recognize that 2000 is a Leap Year and that they, therefore, correctly process transactions and reports over the period from February 28, 2000, to March 1, 2000; and

■ They recognize that 2000 has 366 days and that they, therefore, correctly process transactions and reports over the period December 30, 2000, to January 1, 2001.

**These test routines apply to ALL systems and software in use in your company before modification/conversion, as well as to ALL systems and software that have been modified, converted or newly bought.**

Some basic principles:

■ Don't use live data, i.e., don't test on the data files you use every day. You may copy those files and test on the copies, but make certain the file names are different from those of the files you use every day;

■ Test on a different (spare) machine from the one on which you run your day-to-day applications. Ensure both systems have the same configurations;

■ If you have to use the same machine for testing and live operations, do your tests when live data is not being processed, and ensure that a full back-up has been made; and

■ If your company has not followed a regular policy of backing up systems and checking for viruses, it would be an extremely good idea to start now before you start testing.

## 19.3 Check for this killer in your database files

In existing and new applications, check carefully in the database setup files for any dates which can affect the protection and integrity of your valuable data. For instance, some programs may allow you to keep data on your system up to a"use until" date — at which date all that data is deleted. If your system supports only two-digit dates that date might be 12/31/99, being the last date available.

If the data is unimportant, there's no problem. BUT if it is your customer database or your store's database that gets wiped out, you may have major problems.

## 19.4 Testing and interfaces

Where you transfer data to (and at the request of) a supplier, customer, bank, etc., they will probably notify you of the procedures they want you to follow to test such data transfers so that no problems arise after December 31, 1999.

We suggest that as soon as your inventory has established who your data partners are and how you transmit data back and forth, that you contact all your data partners IMMEDIATELY and start discussing how you will jointly tackle the Year 2000 issue. If you are dealing with a large organization like a bank, which will be establishing a common routine for all its data partners, your role will be to let them know that you are ready and awaiting instructions.

If you are dealing with a smaller organization, it may be appropriate for you to take the lead and initiate full discussions. Your contact may help wake up the owner/manager if potential problems with data transfer have not been given proper consideration.

# 20. The final safety net — a contingency plan

## 20.1 Nobody's perfect — so prepare for trouble

There are various "Laws" (usually with unprintable names) that state that if something can go wrong, it invariably *will*. You must face the fact that you might work vigorously to beat the Year 2000 problem, and still have something go wrong at the last minute. An unexpected glitch in your systems, a customer suddenly going bust, an error in your testing regimes, a long drawn out problem with power or telephone supply .... Or, quite simply, with the best will in the world you and your Year 2000 team might just miss the deadline.

You need to plan for that contingency. Your bank, insurance company and auditors will sooner or later all want to see that not only are you trying to fix your own internal problems, but that you are also planning for all eventualities. Businesses run on routines, and the arrival of computers has helped spread uniform performance, predictability, and order. Until the day that the computers stop being predictable. The day that the computer system tells you that you don't have any stock, despite the fact that a trip to the warehouse shows that this is gibberish ... that no one owes you any money, when you *know* that you are owed tens of thousands ... when it "forgets" that you have valuable orders from your customers in progress, and all the detailed specifications of those orders ... when it loses all the major sales leads that your staff were going to follow up.

Doubtless you can rise above all this if your staff is alert and raise the alarm the instant they suspect something is wrong. But what happens if your staff is used to obeying the computer's orders, having been told that the computer is always right, and sit there believing the information that the computer spews out at them? If this scenario seems far-fetched, then just check out the situation with customers who have disagreed with account statements from utility companies, telephone companies, etc., and have been repeatedly told "the computer says that, so it must be right!"

Which is why you need a contingency plan. This needs to be put in place to deal with a situation in which, despite all your best efforts, matters do not go according to scheme after December 31, 1999.

Any plans are the responsibility of management and must be clearly communicated to all personnel who need to carry them out. You may feel that you require outside expertise — from your auditors, computer suppliers, etc. — to help you put a plan together and to give you a third party perspective.

Begin the contingency plan exercise by first conducting a thorough analysis of the way your business runs — how personnel and computers fit into it and link together. In this analysis, you should also show how you interface to the outside world, whether it be with suppliers, customers, subcontractors, banks, government departments, and so on.

Draw all the connections between departments, the personnel in those departments, and the computers and software that they work with every day. All personnel in your business are concerned with the Year 2000, even if they may not be aware of it yet. Their jobs depend on it. So carry out the analysis as a team effort, getting input from managers and staff.

You need to consider not just the physical routines and methods of doing business, but the business activities involved as well, i.e., how you:

■ Solicit for business (advertising, direct mail, etc.);

- Set up new customers;
- Receive orders;
- Process orders;
- Fulfill orders (manufacture, distribute, etc.);
- Invoice;
- Receive and process payment; and
- Chase for nonpayment (statements, etc.).

The purpose of the contingency plan is to set up a fallback position that assumes that you have been hit by some aspect (or several aspects together) of the Year 2000 problem, and need to cope. This means that your contingency plan CANNOT SIMPLY BE A RETURN TO THE STATUS QUO.

If you have to implement the plan, it will be because some aspects of your business environment have altered dramatically, and trying to turn the clock back will result in failure.

The plan should be designed to click into place as soon as you realize that some of the actions you are taking to beat the Year 2000 problem will not be completed — by which we mean all testing has been finished, and the newly-compliant system is up and running in parallel with your existing computer systems — by June 30, 1999.

This may seem too early, but consider; it is better to meet the new millennium with a well-prepared contingency plan in full swing and with all its teething problems sorted out, than to gamble that you will be able to scramble the last elements of your Year 2000 remedial work into place at the last minute and without making any mistakes. Remember — this is your livelihood we are talking about.

The contingency plan will need to examine whether there are manual systems you could set up to replace computer-based systems that may fail, and similar workarounds.

Bring your staff together, and put various disaster scenarios to them — "what if" brainstorming sessions designed to produce flexible and imaginative thinking. Don't be afraid to discuss these with your staff; if you handle it right, they will see it not as a sign of weakness but of confidence and trust.

And, as we have said, you need their brains and their experience. If you encourage them, they will come up with ideas as to how to cope with the sudden failure of your data partners to receive or transmit material, or the sudden cutting off of key supplies or the collapse of a top customer, or the breakdown of automated systems in your premises or production line.

One last point: remember that any changes you make under the contingency plan, or "quick fixes" you implement, must satisfy your auditor's needs to check that your accounting systems reflect the true financial position of the company.

## 20.2 Make the human factor work for you

Your best weapon in watching for Year 2000 problems is going to be your staff. They need to be extra vigilant for potential errors occurring in, for example, records, invoices, accounts, delivery notes and so on.

Even if you are confident your system is now running smoothly and you expect no hitches, try a brainstorming exercise with your staff to raise a list of what areas of the business need particular checking and double-checking for the period running up to and beyond January 1, 2000.

All supervisors should be briefed on how to incorporate this extra vigilance into their usual daily procedures. You may want to set up a reporting system tailored to the business through which staff report to their supervisors at the end of each day any signs of problems or straws blowing in a millennium wind. Make sure that these reports are scrutinized by the Year 2000 project manager and not just filed in the trash basket.

Draw up a list of priority areas so that attention will immediately be drawn to potential problems in areas most likely to harm the core business. If your employees are kept informed, involved and motivated, they will be your strongest allies at this difficult time. If there is an atmosphere of anxiety where individuals do not feel safe in expressing a nagging concern, then you are in big trouble. Something vital may not be discussed and that could be disastrous for the company.

Your staff may also have to deal with irate customers come the dawn of the new millennium. If they are trained and well-informed, they should be able to handle them; if not, you may lose more customers.

# 21. Conclusion

The Year 2000 problem is not fair.

It is not your fault.

It cannot be dodged.

BUT IT CAN BE BEATEN.

The Year 2000 problem is not mysterious; its causes are understood, the cures well known and certain. The Year 2000 crisis thrives on ignorance, on apathy, on despair. In the face of determination and energy, it will be overcome.

Don't become a victim. Become a victor.

# 22. Sources of help

Now that you have read this guidebook, you should be ready to tackle the Year 2000 issue at once. But this is only the start; you should consider taking these further steps ...

## You Need to Get Management, Partners and Staff Up To Speed

Buy extra copies of this book and spread them around your organization to raise awareness, train, and get your people engaged with the Year 2000 as soon as possible. Check with your local bookstore for quantity discounts or call Kogan Page U.S. at 603-749-9171 or email us at bizbks@aol.com.

## You Need to Spread the Word to Your Suppliers and Customers

Send them copies of this book; consider sending our Year 2000 Survival Packs to key companies in your supply and distribution chains. These can be ordered from Kogan Page U.S. at the number above.

## Start Your Inventory and Letter — Writing Campaigns Now

The Survival Pack contains everything you need to get moving right away:

- An extra copy of *The Millennium Countdown*
- A "Technical Hints and Tips" manual looking at some problems with PCs, spreadsheets, databases, etc.
- 12 different sample letters to send to customers, suppliers, and manufacturers of hardware/software/embedded systems to help you assess the size of your problem
- A diagnostic tool to help you check your PCs
- A disk-based presentation to help your staff, suppliers, etc. understand the problem better (available for Powerpoint, Freelance and DOS)

## Want to Look at the Issue in More Depth?

We can offer you a range of Year 2000 CD-ROMs: Year 2000 Tools and Resources; Year 2000 Testing; Year 2000 Risk Management and Legal Issues.

The Year 2000 Support Centre maintains a substantial Website at http://www.support2000.com, which will help you deal with your Year 2000 problems by giving you access to a whole host of information from official organizations, trade bodies, manufacturers and many others. The site is clearly marked into areas of interest, whether you need technical guidance on the compliance status of your IT systems and equipment, or guidance on business and legal matters, or specific information on how the Year 2000 issue is likely to affect various sectors of industry and commerce, including the financial sector.

For more information on the Year 2000 Support Center you can also email the authors at mike@compinfo.co.uk.

# Appendix One

## United States Small Business Administration Checklists for Small Business

### Y2K Checklists for Small Business

No single Y2K checklist fits everyone's needs since businesses have a wide variety of services and technologies. We are offering several that focus on small business needs, starting with the one below from the Federal Reserve Board. Links to additional checklists, definitions, and resources are provided as well. Keep in mind, there are many excellent checklists on the Internet. Browse the Internet and if you find one you like, let the Small Business Administration know!

### Suggested Steps to Readiness

The most important first step is to develop a strategy to make your business ready for the year 2000. Many consulting firms have developed different strategies from 3 to 15 steps to take to help companies deal with the Year 2000 problem. Information about these different plans can be found on the Internet or in trade journals.

Here is a simple five-step plan to achieve Year 2000 readiness.

## 1) Awareness: educating and involving all levels of your organization in solving the problem.

A crucial step in awareness is creating a communication strategy to make certain that everyone is informed and that management has the information it needs to make decisions. Holding seminars or meetings to educate people and bringing in outside speakers are two ways to increase awareness.

A critical aspect of awareness is to develop an internal standard for Year 2000 readiness. The Federal Reserve uses the following definition: "Systems (e.g., software, hardware, firmware) are defined as ready if they can demonstrate correct management and manipulation of data involving dates, including single-century and multi-century formulas, without causing an abnormally ended scenario within the system or generating incorrect values involving such dates."

The awareness phase never ends. As people move to other jobs, and new people are hired, they must be educated. There is also an ongoing need to keep your staff and business partners informed.

### 2) Inventory: creating your checklist toward Year 2000 readiness

In this phase, you should identify and list all of the different computer-based systems, components (such as in-house developed systems, purchased software, computers and associated hardware), service providers, and hardware that contains microchips that support your business. Each entry on your list should be ranked by how critical it is to your business.

Indicate on your inventory whether the component is hardware, software, or a service. It may be useful to note which components support your telephone or data communications networks. If a computer-based system uses a vendor-supplied package, record the name of the vendor and the release number, if known.

**Hint:** Keeping your inventory on a spreadsheet or database makes it easier to sort and report on items that are not ready. It is also helpful to develop an identification system to help track components. For each item on the inventory, assign a person who will be responsible for assessing that item and preparing it for the year 2000.

**Reminder:** Some systems will begin failing before the century date changes because they perform forecasting or future processing. This is called "time horizon to failure" and should be considered during inventory and assessment. The "time horizon to failure" should be listed on your inventory if it is known.

### 3) Assessment: examining how severe and widespread the problem is in your business and what needs to be fixed

Starting with the most critical items on the inventory, determine which systems are date-sensitive and if they will fail when the century changes. Systems with an imminent "time horizon to failure" should also be assessed first. A date-sensitive system is one that manipulates or works with dates in some way, or a system that operates differently based upon the date.

Examples of date-sensitive systems include ones that perform any kind of forecasting or projections through time, such as calculating interest on a loan or projecting inventory levels. Other examples of date-sensitive systems are those which retrieve records based on a date (such as invoices), or systems that sort items by date (such as accounting or inventory systems). Examples of date-sensitive hardware include lighting systems that switch on automatically on weekdays, manufacturing control systems, and scanners or card readers that read ID badges or credit/debit cards.

One way to assess a system is to look at the computer code and follow the logic. If this is not possible because the system is based on a purchased package, you should contact the vendor.

Another way to assess a system is to run it as if it were already the year 2000. Running the system with dates other than the current date may require resetting the system date. There are risks involved in resetting system dates. Each organization should evaluate the impact of resetting system dates. This testing may require that your test data be "aged" properly so it contains the correct internal dates.

**Hint:** There are risks involved in rolling the dates on your computer systems forward. Make sure you understand what these risks are for your organization.

For some specialized systems, such as building or manufacturing control systems, or systems with embedded microchips, you may need to have the vendor work with your staff to test and assess the system.

Once you have determined the state of readiness for each system and component listed in your inventory, you should develop a strategy for dealing with those systems that have to be fixed. There are only three possible strategies: repair, replace, or retire the system.

If you decide to repair a system, there are two possible repair strategies or approaches: windowing or date expansion. The date expansion strategy involves expanding all two-digit year fields in your system's data files and in the programs that process those files so they can hold the century as well as the two-digit year. For example, a two-digit year fields YY might be expanded to a four-digit CCYY field, where CC is the century. The date expansion may involve increasing the size of files that hold your data.

The windowing approach involves inserting logic into your programs that interprets year fields to determine what century the year falls into before the date field is used in calculations, comparisons or sorting. Here is an example of this logic: if the year is between 00 and 49, the century is 20, otherwise the century is 19. This is called the 50 year window. There are other windows. You need to determine which one is appropriate for your particular system. Whatever windowing logic is selected, we recommend using it consistently throughout your organization to avoid later error and confusion.

Most businesses are taking a mixed approach, fixing some systems using windowing logic and others with date expansion. Some are using such a mixed approach to fix even large systems. Your choice depends on your own individual needs.

If your strategy is to replace a nonready system, you have several choices. You can build the replacement in-house (or hire contractors to work with your staff to build it), you can purchase a replacement system from a vendor, or you can outsource that particular line of business to a service bureau or other outside service provider. It is very important to determine when the replacement will be ready. If the replacement won't be tested and installed until after the "time horizon to failure," you may be forced into a repair strategy.

A business system that operates in isolation is very rare. Most interface with other business systems to exchange data, and some interface with systems outside your organization. Your strategy to replace or repair nonready systems should take into account those systems' interfaces with other systems, both within and outside your organization. For example, if you opt for date expansion, you must consider the impact of sending larger files to all interfaces. If you opt for windowing, all interfaces must be informed of the window scheme.

**Hint:** We recommend that you develop a chart that shows all the systems that interface with others, what those interfaces are and when they occur.

Different systems that interface with each other may have different schedules for assessment, correction, and implementation. It may be necessary to build "bridges" between systems that are ready for the year 2000 and those that are not. These bridges, which are usually temporary programs, take data from one system and modify it to make the format correct for the interfacing system. Careful, detailed planning will be required to handle these situations.

When you find that a system is not year 2000 ready, determine how critical that system is to your business. For example, if the system prints an invalid date on an internally used report, you may decide that this problem is not significant to address. If, however, the system loses track of inventory data or fails to forecast properly, it should be fixed.

**Hint:** As you purchase new computers, packages, and other hardware; upgrade existing packages, and develop new lines of business, remember that this new equipment needs to be checked to ensure it is year 2000 ready. Upgraded packages also need to be checked for readiness after upgrading.

**Correction and Testing: implementing the readiness strategy you have chosen and testing the fix.**

Testing is a critical aspect of any Year 2000 project. Testing verifies that the repaired or replaced system operates properly when the date changes and that existing business functions (such as accounting, inventory control, and order tracking) continue to operate as expected. Testing also verifies that interfacing systems are not adversely affected. You should not confine your testing efforts solely to computer programs. Other systems (including network operating systems, vendor-supplied software, building infrastructure systems, PCs, and components with embedded microchips) should be tested to ensure they will not fail when the century changes.

There are several critical tests you should perform once you've changed or replaced a system. The best way to see if a system is ready for the year 2000 is to test the system as if it were already the year 2000. Test that the system will operate correctly after the date has rolled over from 12/31/1999 to 1/1/2000. Because the year 2000 is a leap year, you should test that your system will recognize 2/29/2000 as a valid date and that it will roll over from 2/28/2000 to 2/29/2000, and from 2/29/2000 to 3/1/2000. You should also test your fixed system with a date before 2000 to ensure that it works. See "Suggested Testing Criteria" for other suggested dates to test on your system.

**Warning:** There are risks involved in rolling dates forward on computers. Some computer security systems keep track of the last time a user accessed a system and will revoke or inactivate that user's password if it has not accessed the system for a period of time. Rolling the date forward may cause user passwords to be inactivated by the security system. Data sets that should be retained may be marked as expired and could be written over. Some software packages may be leased and you may be paying an annual fee to the vendor. Rolling the date past the end of the lease may cause the software package to freeze up or generate error messages.

There are several other tests that you may want to carry out, depending on the functions your system supports. If your system does end-of-the-week, end-of-the-month, and end-of-the-quarter and/or end-of-year processing, these should be tested. You should test that the system will forecast and retrieve data properly. Set the date to a date in 1999 and check that the system will forecast into the next century. Set the system to a date in the 21st century (any date after 12/31/1999) and test that the system will retrieve historical data from some period before 12/31/1999.

**Hint:** Whenever possible, testing should be carried out in a test environment to minimize the chance of corrupting the production systems. Also, be careful changing historical or backup files if you choose date expansion. You may lose an important audit trail. We suggest you consult with your auditors and legal staff before changing historical or backup files.

**Definition:** The term "product environment" refers to the set of hardware and software that supports your day-to-day operations. "Test environment" refers to the hardware and software where new or changed systems can be tested without disturbing your day-to-day operations.

**Hint:** Testing of changed systems should be carried out in an environment that is ready for the year 2000. You should work with your vendors to determine when their hardware platforms will be compliant and use those dates to build your test plans. If your vendor cannot supply the platform in time to meet your schedule, you should be aware of the risks involved and be prepared to retest your changed system once the platform is ready.

**Implementation: moving your repaired or replaced system into your production environment.**

Before you install your replacement or repaired system, you should develop an installation plan and contingency plans. The installation plan lists all the files and programs that need to be moved into production, and all the steps to make your changed system work. Your installation plan may include testing in production to ensure that the installed systems are working as expected. Contingency plans list the possible problems that you can foresee and what steps you will take if these problems occur.

**Hint:** You may want to make backups of the production files from the old system. If possible, you may want to install the ready system and run it in parallel with the old system and compare results.

**Reminder:** Your contingency plans should not include reverting to the old system. The old system is not ready for the year 2000, otherwise you would not be replacing or repairing it.

**Warning:** In planning to replace a system, make certain that you allow enough time to replace all of the necessary pieces of that system

Don't get contaminated.

Once your have repaired your systems and made them year 2000 compliant, you should take steps to make sure that subsequent changes do not contaminate those systems by introducing year 2000 bugs. A system might get contaminated if a programmer makes changes to a repaired system and inadvertently changes the logic that handles the century change. A vendor-supplied package might also become contaminated if subsequent releases of the package don't include the year 2000 changes.

Retest the year 2000 changes as part of any subsequent system modification effort. We recommend that you save the test data and test cases that were used to test the original changes and use them whenever you are testing other changes to that system. This is called regression testing. We also suggest that any new releases of vendor-supplied packages also be year 2000 tested.

## Personal Computers

Today personal computers are widely used in many businesses. All personal computers have an internal clock/calendar that maintains and reports the date and time. In some computers, the year is stored and processed as two rather than four digits. The year 2000 will affect these computers just as it affects other systems. If you are running systems on your computers that access that PCs date, these systems may fail or produce bad results. All PCs should be tested, regardless of how they are used.

The following section, "How to Check a Personal Computer for Year 2000 Readiness," lists the steps you can follow to test your personal computer. You can also run PC test software that is available on the Internet.

Take an organized approach to this problem. List all your PCs, test them for readiness, and mark those that are not ready for later attention. Bright fluorescent labels can be used to mark PCs as ready or not.

There are several possible ways to correct this PC date problem. You may contact a computer retailer to investigate purchasing a new Basic Input/Output System (BIOS) chip that is year 2000 ready, download software solutions from the Internet, or replace the non-ready PC with a model that is Year 2000 ready.

**Hint:** Anytime you reset the date on a PC, you run the risk of corrupting your system. You can minimize the risk either by backing up all of the critical files or by resetting the date in a test environment. Don't forget to reset the date to the correct date/time after you have tested the system. If you are testing a LAN file server, power off all of the workstations connected to that LAN before going through the date test procedure.

**Warning:** Even a brand-new state-of-the-art PC may not be ready for the year 2000. New PCs should be tested before they are installed.

### Your business is NOT alone

No business exists in a vacuum. Yours is part of a chain of customers, suppliers, utilities, and vendors. Year 2000 failures in any of these can impact your business. Here are some tips to protect your business within this chain.

**Vendor-supplied products:** Many software vendors were caught by surprise by the year 2000 problem and some will not be able to make their products ready for it. Others may make their products ready but may not be able to deliver the ready software until late 1999. Some vendors may no longer support a particular product that you may be running, and other vendors may have gone out of business.

For date-sensitive systems, contact the vendors to find out their readiness plans. If a vendor will not give you information about the readiness status of a package, or if a Year 2000-ready version will not be available until late in 1999, you should investigate an alternative system. Even if a vendor insists its product can handle the century date change, you still should test and certify it to your satisfaction. If the vendor insists that an upgraded version of a program package is ready, that package still must be tested since the vendor and you may have different definitions of readiness.

**Data processing service bureaus:** If you use a service bureau for your data processing needs, contact it to discuss its plans for year 2000 readiness.

Make a list of all the services provided by your service bureau, ranking them according to how critical they are to your business, and then contact the service bureau in writing about each service. If a service bureau says it is ready for the year 2000, ask it to provide test results demonstrating this. If possible, test the service for yourself. If it is ready for certain services but not for others, you should determine what this means to your business. Decide if there is a "work around" you can implement. If the service bureau says it will have a Year 2000 version in the future, you need to assess what that means to your business. A date late in 1999 may be too risky.

**Utilities and services:** If your local utility fails to provide you with water, gas, or electricity, your buildings will not be usable and your business will suffer. You should contact all companies that provide essential services such as janitorial, repair, delivery, etc. You should contact all of your suppliers to discuss the state of their Year 2000 readiness and make contingency plans.

**Record storage/retention firms:** You may use a firm to store critical legal documents and backup tapes offsite. These firms should be contacted to determine their state of readiness. It could be disastrous if you have an emergency and discover that your offsite storage firm can't find your backups.

## Other Sources of Help

There are many helpful sources you can turn to for making your business ready for the century date change. The Internet has thousands of web sites dedicated to the Year 2000 problem. Many sites have links to sources of freeware, planning tools, discussion groups and so forth.

Here is a short list of useful Web sites.

http://www.year2000.com — Peter de Jager's Web site: good source of links to other sites

http://www.compinfo.co.uk/y2k/manufpos.html — contains links to computer manufacturer's home pages where you can find Year 2000 compliance information.

http://www.software.ibm.com/year2000/ — IBM's year 2000 page.

http://www.microsoft.com/smallbiz/edge/yr2000/default.htm — Microsoft's Year 2000 page.

http://www.gmt-2000.com/gmt-2000/homepage_frameset.html — the link to Greenwich Mean Time's home page with evaluations of PC testers and BIOS chips — useful for PC evaluation.

http://pw2.netcom.com/~helliott/00.htm — The so-called "Mother of all Y2K link sites" contains many links to other sites.

http://www.jks.co.uk/y2k/confer/notices/dtisme01.htm — link to a report "Helping the Small Business Tackle Year 2000."

http://www.isquare.com/y2k.htm — The Small Business Advisor Web site.

http://www.bog.frb.fed.us/y2k/ — The Year 2000 page of the Board of Governors of the Federal Reserve Bank.

http://www.ffiec.gov/y2k/ — The Year 2000 page of the Federal Financial Institutions Examination Council.

http://www.frbsf.org/fiservices/cdc — The Federal Reserve Bank of San Francisco's Year 2000 page.

Personal organizations or trade associations may be able to provide you with support and advice. There are many consulting firms and independent consultants who can help you get your business ready for the century date change. Many data processing and business magazines have articles about the Year 2000 problem and most large cities now have Year 2000 user groups that meet to discuss the problem. One magazine that is dedicated solely to the Year 2000 problem is called *The Year 2000 Journal*. The *Journal* can be reached at (214) 340-2147; its Internet address is http://www.y2kjournal.com.

If you can't find a year 2000 user group in your area, form one. It can become your support group and someone in your group may have already solved problems that you are facing. If you form or join a year

2000 user group, invite local political officials to become involved. They will have to work with their local government agencies to ensure that police and fire services, water, electricity and other utilities are uninterrupted.

## Some questions to help assess system readiness

- Can the system perform projections through time? For example, can it calculate interest of payments or make inventory projections?

- Does the system allow for entering dates? If yes, is the year indicated by 2 or 4 digits? What happens if you enter "00" or "01"?

- Will the system operate differently depending on the day of the week? Will it operate differently at month-end, quarter-end or year-end?

- Can the system put things in order by date?

- Does the system have a security feature that includes date checking?

- Can the system perform data-based calculations?

- Does the system have a security feature that includes date checking?

## Suggested Testing Criteria

The following list is not all inclusive. You should add others based on your business's needs and ignore those that are not appropriate.

Test the changed system with dates before the year 2000 to ensure that it is working properly.

Test that the changed system properly rolls over from 12/31/1999 to 1/1/2000.

Validate the first business day of the year 2000 (1/1/2000, 1/2/2000, etc., depending on your business needs).

Validate that the system operates correctly at end-of-the-month (1/31/2000 and will roll over to 2/1/2000 properly).

Test that the system rolls over from 2/28/2000 to 2/29/2000 properly, operates correctly on 2/29/2000, then rolls over and operates properly on 3/1/2000.

Test 3/31/2000 and 4/1/2000 to show that end-of-quarter processing operates correctly.

Test 1/7/2000 and 1/10/2000 to insure that the system operates correctly on the first Friday of the new century and on the Monday after the first Friday.

Validate year display fields, including data entry.

Validate the year in reports.

Test that the system sorts in correct order, validate all sort processing.

Validate correct calculation of dates.

Validate the correct acceptance of dates from the operating systems.

Validate calculated resultant values from dates.

Test that ages are calculated correctly.

Validate interest and other time-based financial calculations.

Test expiration date processing.

Test historical decision analysis

Validate time reporting processing.

Test workflow/materials requisition and inventory processing.

Verify that billing calculations are correct.

Validate cycle processing, including day-of-week and/or first business day of the month.

Verify that the system forecasts correctly.

Test forward processing — process dates after the year 2000 (2001, 2002, etc.).

Validate backward processing — process dates prior to 2000.

Verify historical or archival date processing.

Validate that the system purges the correct records.

Validate date and data error handling routines.

Validate date expansion, if used, both within the application and between interfacing applications.

Validate windowing, if used, both within the system and between interfacing systems.

Validate proper handling of special values in dates — 99/99/9999, 88/88/8888, 00/00/0000.

Validate that the system works with the date 1/1/1999 — first date with "99" in the year field.

Validate that there are 366 days in the year 2000, and 365 days in the year 2001.

Validate that 9/9/99 (September 9, 1999) is handled properly.

## Some additional dates that may impact businesses

7/1/1999: This is when 46 out of 50 states start their Fiscal Year 2000.

10/1/1999: The start of Federal Government's Fiscal Year 2000.

2/15/2000: W2s due.

4/15/2000: Tax day.

4/30/2000: First month ending in a weekend.

5/1/2000: Tax withholding reports due, unemployment tax due.

9/30/2000: Federal Government's end of Fiscal Year 2000.

10/10/2000:˙ First "six-digit" date for systems storing date as MDDYY.

12/31/2000 (Sunday): First year end — check that year contains 366 days.

1/1/2001: Test that the system has been instructed to roll over to 2001.

2/29/2001: Invalid date.

12/31/2001: Second year end — check that year has 365 days.

## How to Check a Personal Computer for Year 2000 Readiness

The following test is suggested to determine if a personal computer will roll over to the year 2000 correctly.

The test presented here requires a bootable DOS floppy diskette. This is a safe method to test your PCs system clock because it leaves the data and programs on your PCs hard disk unaffected. If you boot to your C: drive, you may end up loading Windows or Windows 95 and other applications from your start-up routine. Using a bootable diskette will ensure the integrity of the data and programs on your PCs hard disks. The test script presented here will check your PCs ability to transition to the year 2000 and recognize it as a leap year.

Don't perform the tests by changing your system's BIOS Setup screen.

Create a bootable test diskette. Insert a blank floppy diskette into the PCs A: drive. From a DOS prompt, type FORMAT A:/S. Or from Windows File Manager, click on DISK/FORMAT and check MAKE SYSTEM DISK.

With the bootable diskette you created that is still in your PCs floppy drive, shut down your system (close Windows) and then power off your PC. Don't just hit the reset button or warmboot (CTL-ALT-DEL).

Power on your PC, and allow the PC to boot from the diskette.

After bootup, DOS automatically shows the current date. Make sure that the correct date is displayed. Otherwise, you may have to set the correct date on your PCs BIOS.

At the Enter new date (mm/dd/yy) prompt, type 12/31/1999.

After changing the date, the current time will be displayed. At the Enter new time prompt, type 23:55:00.

Turn the power off on your PC and wait at least 10 minutes. If you don't, DOS will appear to transition correctly to the year 2000. However, once you reboot the PC, it will display the incorrect date if your system's RTC has the flaw described above.

Turn the power back on and wait for the boot process to complete.

Type in Date at the ready prompt. If Sat 01-01-2000 is displayed, your PCs BIOS passes the test.

At the Enter new date (mm/dd/yy) prompt, type 2/28/2000. This will test your system's ability to recognize the year 2000 as a leap year.

After changing the date, the current time will be displayed. At the Enter new time prompt, type 23:55:00.

Power off your PC again and wait at least 10 minutes.

Power on the PC. Type in Date at the Ready prompt. If Tue 02/29/2000 appears, your PCs BIOS passes the leap year test.

To conclude testing, at the Enter new date (mm-dd-yy) prompt, enter the correct date.

After changing the date, the current time will be displayed. At the Enter new time prompt, type correct time.

Remove the bootable diskette from the floppy and power off your PC.

# Appendix Two

## Sample Year 2000 Compliance Agreement

**Year 2000 Compliance Agreement**
Supplied by: Timothy J. Feathers
Hillix, Brewer, Hoffhaus, Whittaker & Wright, L.L.C.
2420 Pershing Road, 4th floor
Kansas City, Missouri 64108
816-221-0355
816-421-2896 (fax)

---

**Note:** NOBODY takes responsibility for how you use this document. You are strongly advised to consult with your own legal counsel in all legal matters. This is reproduced only to serve as an example of what might be included in a Y2K compliance agreement.

---

**THE COMPLIANCE AGREEMENT** is made by and between
_____("Licensee") and
_____("Licensor") effective as of the
___ day of ____ 199__

### RECITAL

**WHEREAS**, Licensor and Licensee are parties to that certain Software License Agreement dated 19___ (the "License Agreement); and

**WHEREAS**, Licensee has requested that Licensor provide additional warranties regarding the Software particularly regarding Year 2000 Compliance (as hereafter defined); and

**WHEREAS**, Licensor is willing to provide the requested warranties on the terms and conditions set forth in this Agreement.

**NOW, THEREFORE**, in consideration of the Recitals, the continuation of the relationship between Licensor and Licensee, the mutual promises and agreements set forth in the License Agreement, and herein, and for the sum of One Hundred Dollars and other good and valuable consideration, the receipt and sufficiency of which are acknowledged, the parties hereto agree as follows:

1. Year 2000 Compliance

- 1.1 Licensor represents and warrants that the Software is designed to be used prior to, during, and after the calendar year 2000 A.D., and that the Software will operate during each such time period without error relating to date data, specifically including any error relating to, or the product of, date data which represents or references different centuries or more than one century.

- Without limiting the generality of the foregoing, Licensor further represents and warrants:

  - That the Software will not abnormally end or provide invalid or incorrect results as a result of date data, specifically including date data which represents or references different centuries or more than one century;

  - That the Software has been designed to ensure year 2000 compatibility, including, but not limited to, date data century recognition, calculations which accommodate same century and multi-century formulas and date values, and date data interface values that reflect the century;

  - That the software includes "year 2000 capabilities." For the purposes of this Agreement, "year 2000 capabilities" means the Software:

    a) will manage and manipulate data involving dates, includ-
ing single century formulas and multi-century formulas,
and will not cause an abnormally ending scenario within
the application or generate incorrect values or invalid
results involving such dates; and

    b) provides that all date-related user interface functionali-
ty's and data fields include the indication of century; and

    c) provides that all date-related data interface functionali-
ty's include the indication of century.

- The term "Year 2000 Compliance Warranty" shall mean, col-
lectively, the warranties set forth in this Section 1.

2. Term. The Year 2000 Compliance Warranty set forth herein shall
begin as of the date of the License Agreement and end on the
date after January 1, 2000, subsequent to which the Software has
operated without a breach of the Year 2000 Compliance
Warranty for a consecutive six month period.

3. Waiver of Limitation of Liability. Any provisions of the License
Agreement which tend to limit or eliminate the liability of either
party shall have no application with respect to the Year 2000
Compliance Warranty set forth herein.

4. Limitation on Use/Limitation on Liability. In the event that
Licensee is entitled to modify the software pursuant to the
License Agreement, Licensee agrees that it shall not modify the
Software in any manner which would affect the performance of
the Software in such a manner as to cause it to fail to meet the
Year 2000 Compliance Warranty set forth herein. There shall
be no liability on the part of Licensor for any failure of the
Software to conform to the Year 2000 Compliance Warranty to
the extent that any such failure is attributable to a modification
of the Software by Licensee.

5. Provisions of Compliance Agreement Controlling. In the event
of any conflict or apparent conflict between the terms and conditions of the License Agreement and the terms and conditions
of this Compliance Agreement, the terms and conditions of this

Compliance Agreement shall control. Except to the extent otherwise set forth herein, the terms and conditions of the License Agreement shall remain in full force and effect.

6. Entire Agreement. This Compliance Agreement, together with the License Agreement, constitutes the entire agreement between the parties with respect to the subject matter hereof. This Compliance Agreement shall not be modified except by later written agreement signed by both parties.

**IN WITNESS WHEREOF** the parties have executed this Agreement the day and date first set forth above.

## Year 2000 Warranty

**Note:** NOBODY takes responsibility for how you use this document. You are strongly advised to consult with your own legal counsel in all legal matters. This is reproduced only to serve as an example of what might be included in a Y2K Warranty.

1. Licensor represents and warrants that the Software is designed to be used prior to, during, and after the calendar year 2000 A.D., and that the Software will operate during each such time period without error relating to date data, specifically including any error relating to, or the product of, date data which represents or references different centuries or more than one century.

2. Without limiting the generality of the foregoing, Licensor further represents and warrants:

   a. That the Software will not abnormally end or provide invalid or incorrect results as a result of date data, specifically including date data which represents or references different centuries or more than one century;

   b. That the Software has been designed to ensure year 2000 compatibility, including, but not limited to, date data century recognition, calculations which accommodate same century and multi-century formulas and date values, and date data interface values that reflect the century;

   c. That the software includes "year 2000 capabilities." For the purposes of this Agreement, "year 2000 capabilities" means the Software:

      - will manage and manipulate data involving dates, including single century formulas and multi-century formulas, and will not cause an abnormally ending scenario within the application or generate incorrect values or invalid results involving such dates; and

      - provides that all date-related user interface functionality's and data fields include the indication of century; and

- provides that all date-related data interface functionality's include the indication of century.

## 1. Definitions

Four Digit Year Format
shall mean a format that allows entry or processing of a four digit year date: the first two digits will designate the century and the second two digits shall designate the year within the century. As an example, 1996 shall mean the 96th year of the 20th century.

Leap Year
shall mean the year during which an extra day is added in February (February 29th). Leap Year occurs in all years divisible by 400 or evenly divisible by 4 and not evenly divisible by 100. For example, 1996 is a Leap Year since it is divisible by 4 and not evenly divisible by 100. 2000 is a Leap Year since it is divisible by 400.

Year 2000 Compliant
shall mean that the data outside of the range 1990–1999 will be correctly processed in any level of computer hardware or software including, but not limited to, microcode, firmware, application programs, files and databases.

2. **Year 2000 Compliance Performance Warranty** Licensor further warrants and represents that the Product is and will continue to be Year 2000 Compliant. All date processing by Product will include Four Digit Year Format and recognize and correctly process dates for Leap Year. Additionally, all date sorting by Product that includes a "year category" shall be done based on the Four Digit Year Format code.

3. **Remedies for Non-Compliance of Warranty** Licensor agrees to pay liquidated damages in the amount of $_____ per day for each day the Product fails to maintain and uphold the Year 2000 Compliance Performance Warranty described in Section of this Agreement.

## Year 2000 Warranties

**Licensor represents and warrants that:**

- The Software will function without error or interruption in relation to date data, specifically including errors or interruptions from functions which may involve date data from more than one century;

- The Software requires that all date data (whether received from users, systems, applications or other sources) include an indication of century in each instance;

- All date output and results, in any form, shall include an indication of century in each instance.

When used in this Section, the term "date data" shall mean any data or input which includes an indication of or reference to date. The foregoing is in addition to the other representations and warranties set forth herein.

# Appendix Three

## *Inc.* Magazine's Year 2000 Web Links

The best places online to go for more information, products, and help about the year 2000. *Inc.* Magazine's Web site, www.inc.com, lists a number of links that will provide more information. Look under the "Year 2000 Web Links" section.

**Year 2000 Information Center:** Millennium Bug Guru Peter de Jager's page is one of the useful resources on the Web. Included are news, articles, hardware and software updates, user groups, job listings and more.

**Information Technology Association of America Year 2000 Buyer's Guide:** Basic information on the Y2K problem and where software tools can help.

**2K-Times:** Articles, links, and papers written about the millennium.

**Legal and Management Information on the Y2K Problem:** A Web site dedicated to legal advice for your year 2000 problem.

**Millennium Rollover:** The Year 2000 Problem: How to Formulate a Prevention Plan.

**The Gartner Group:** Year 2000 statistics and advice.

**FAQ about the Year 2000 Crisis:** A concise list of answers, in laymen's terms, to the frequently asked questions about the problem.

**CIO's Year 2000 Resource Center:** Advice, information and a conference for information technology executives.

**Ten Management and Legal Pitfalls:** A list of 10 questions about your company and liability.

**Year 2000 Related Books:** Online bookstore dedicated to Millennium Bug titles.

**Year 2000 Management Briefing:** Downloadable Y2K awareness training system.

**Ed Yourdon's Home Page:** Chapters from Yourdon's soon-to-be-released book.

**ITANZ Year 2000:** A reference library and information on certification, software and compliance, and service providers.

**Tick, tick, tick...:** A newsletter for Millennial management.

**Year 2000 Computer Failures:** Managing the Business and Legal Risks: forewarned and forearmed — preparing your business for what could go wrong.

**Legal Considerations Links Page:** Links to various sites covering legal issues from liability to warranty language.

**Vendor Liability and the Year 2000 Crisis:** Who is responsible when things go wrong.

**Computer Software and Year 2000 Compliance:** How to know whether your technology is compliant and what to do if it is not.

**Next Millennium Consulting:** A risk management consulting firm dealing exclusively with the year 2000 problem.

Reprinted with permission of *Inc.* magazine, Goldhirsh Group, Inc., 38 Commercial Wharf, Boston, MA 02110 (http://www.inc.com). *Year 2000 Web Links* (Inc. Web Site), Inc. Staff, 11/18/97. Reproduced by permission of the publisher via Copyright Clearance Center, Inc.

# Appendix Four

## Sample Year 2000 Vendor Certification Questionnaire

### Year 2000 Vendor Certification Questionnaire

| Vendor Name: | Questionnaire Completed By: *(please print/type legibly)* |
|---|---|
| Date Complete: | Completed By *(please sign)* |
| Contact Phone#: | |

    Name of Company   "Year 2000 Compliant" means that the product, software, data files, or services you provide will:

- Properly process or otherwise utilize dates beyond December 31, 1999;
- Be able to correctly recognize February 29, 2000 (the year 2000 is a leap year)

Please answer the following questions using the above definition of Year 2000 Compliance:

| # | Question | Response |
|---|----------|----------|
| 1. | Are the product(s) and/or service(s) you provide us currently Year 2000 compliant under this definition? | |
| 2. | If the model, version, or release of the product or service currently provided is not Year 2000 compliant, please provide the model, version, or release that will properly process these dates. | |
| 3. | If the model, version, or release that is Year 2000 compliant is not yet ready please provide us the date when it will be available. *The upgraded product or service must be available early enough to provide our organization sufficient time to test it and make any necessary changes due to its impact on any internally developed systems, etc.* | |
| 4. | If the model of the product or service provided is not currently Year 2000 compliant as defined above, please tell us what impact this will have on the product or service's performance if it is not made compliant. | |
| 5. | If you are a service provider, have you completed a project to ensure that all of your computer hardware or software, other equipment with date sensitive embedded microchips, and other suppliers and service *continued* | |

| # | Question | Response |
|---|----------|----------|
| 5. | providers will be able to properly handle these dates? If not, on what date can you commit to having this project completed? | |
| 6. | Are all dates used in your product converted to four digit years? | |
| 7. | If not, please include a description of the date formats that will be supported as input and/or output from your product, if applicable. | |
| 8. | Is windowing or field expansion being used or planned? | |
| 9. | If windowing is used, what is the key year — 70? 80? Other? | |
| 10. | Are there prerequisite or corequisite changes needed of us for you to be able to comply? If so, please specify. | |
| 11. | Are there any product components not under your control? If so, how will these components be made compliant? | |
| 12. | If your product or service is already Year 2000 compliant or you have an active effort to become compliant, how did you test or how do you plan to test the product or service to certify compliance? Did an outside company assist you in testing? What tools were used in testing, if any? | |

| # | Question | Response |
|---|----------|----------|
| 13. | Can you provide references or other evidence that you will be able to correctly process these dates? Did an outside company certify your Year 2000 effort? | |
| 14. | Does your product or service use any "time bombs" which would prevent us from future testing with dates after the millennium? If not, please provide us with instructions about how we would conduct Year 2000 compliance testing of your product or service. | |
| 15. | Has your organization purchased any business interruption or other insurance to mitigate against losses incurred for non-compliance with Year 2000 issues? If so, please provide us with a certification of this Year 2000 insurance coverage. | |
| 16. | As part of your vendor management process, have you developed contingency plans in the event that one of your important suppliers or service providers is not Year 2000 compliant by your committed target date for being compliant? | |
| 17. | Finally, to assist us in evaluating your efforts, please provide us with the following information:<br>• Estimate of total expense to correct all Year 2000 problems<br><br>*continued* | |

| # | Question | Response |
|---|----------|----------|
| 17. | • Number of lines of program code to be corrected (or were corrected) to be Year 2000 compliant.<br><br>• Number of Full Time Equivalent (FTE) staff dedicated to Year 2000 project. | |

# Appendix Five

## A Checklist of Computer Systems and Applications

Check in your own organization where dates are used in the following departmental applications (add to, and delete from, the list, as necessary). Ask the users where they use dates in screen displays and in reports. Ask where they pass date information to another user, internal or external, (or back to the mainframe) or where they receive information from another user, internal or external (or from the mainframe).

☐ Accounting

☐ Contracts

☐ Databases

☐ Desktop/notebook

☐ PDA applications

☐ Help desk

☐ Maintenance

☐ Marketing

☐ Operational

☐ Contact managers/organizers

☐ Credit control

☐ Decision support

☐ Direct mail

☐ Distribution

☐ Legal

☐ Manufacturing

☐ Membership/loyalty schemes

☐ Order processing

☐ Payroll        ☐ Personnel

☐ Spreadsheets     ☐ Stock control

☐ Transport       ☐ Warehousing

# Appendix Six

## An Overview and Checklist of Embedded Systems and Process Control Systems

### An overview of embedded systems
By The Institution of Electrical Engineers

### What is an embedded system?

A general purpose definition of embedded systems is that they are devices used to control, monitor or assist the operation of equipment, machinery or plant. "Embedded" reflects the fact that they are an integral part of the system. In many cases their very embedded nature may be such that their presence is far from obvious to the casual observer, and even the more technically skilled might need to examine the operation of a piece of equipment for some time before being able to conclude that an embedded control device was involved in its functioning. At the other extreme a general purpose computer may be used to control the operation of a large complex processing plant, and its presence will be obvious.

All embedded systems are computers. Some of them are, however, very simple devices compared with a PC. The simplest devices consist of a single microprocessor (often called a "chip") which may itself be packaged with other chips in a hybrid or Application Specific Integrated Circuit (ASIC). Its input comes from a detector or sensor and its output goes to a switch or activator which (for example) may start or stop the operation of a machine or, by operating a valve, may control the flow of fuel to an engine.

128

The very simplest embedded systems are capable of performing only a single function or set of functions to meet a single predetermined purpose. In the more complex systems, the functioning of the embedded system is determined by an application program which enables the embedded system to do things for a specific application. The ability to have programs means that the same system can be used for a variety of different purposes. In some cases a microprocessor may be designed in such a way that application software for a particular purpose can be added to the basic software in a second process, after which it is not possible to make further changes: this is sometimes referred to as firmware.

## Embedded systems compared with commercial systems

The Year 2000 problem in embedded systems differs from the problem in commercial/database/transaction processing systems (often referred to as IT systems) in a number of ways.

Firstly, the user's problem may much lie much deeper than is the case with packages or applications software. It may lie in — and be inseparable from — systems and operating software and from hardware, i.e., in the platform on which the application software is based. When users of IT systems have hardware or operating software problems they can, and should, be made the concern of the computer supplier; typically, this is not the case with microprocessors and devices based on them.

Secondly, in embedded systems the concern is often with intervals rather than with specific dates: the need may be for an event to occur at 100-day intervals rather than on the fifth day of each month. This has the implication that Year 2000 problems may reveal themselves both before and for some time after 1 January 2000, and not at all on the date itself. On the other hand there is a possibility that devices with cycles which are measured in hours and minutes, or even seconds, may be affected by the problem because year numbers are the basis of time calculations. In such systems the effect may not be evident on (as it were) the stroke of midnight but will arise sometime during the following 24 hours.

## Categories of embedded systems and Year 2000 risks

Any or all of these may be in your plant and equipment and in your products.

- ■ Individual microprocessors;
- ■ Small assemblies of microprocessors with no timing function;
- ■ Subassemblies with a timing function; and/or
- ■ Computer systems used in manufacturing or process control.

### Individual microprocessors

These may be found in small devices such as temperature sensors, smoke and gas detectors, circuit breakers, etc. It is highly unlikely — but nevertheless possible — that these will be affected. If they are, (1) it will not be evident after the date and (2) the only possible action is to replace the microprocessor. If in doubt you should consult the supplier.

### Small assemblies of microprocessors with no timing function

These may be found in flow controllers, signal amplifiers, position sensors and valve actuators. It is unlikely that these will be affected. However, they may depend on a clock for their internal operation which might be affected by the Year 2000 problem. This is unlikely to reveal itself before the date. If you suspect there may be a problem, you should consult the supplier.

### Subassemblies with a timing function

Special devices such as switchgear, controllers (e.g. for traffic), telephone exchanges, elevators, data acquisition and monitoring systems, diagnostic and real time control systems, may fall into this category. These systems may be local elements in a larger system to which they pass data collected from their sensors. They may incorporate a PC, and may involve some kind of database (e.g., of events). In these the Year 2000 problem may affect: their systems or application software, the database, and the networks and data transmission systems they use to communicate with the larger system. The error may become apparent before 2000 (because the system may attempt to make a record of when next a particular action should take place), on the date 01/01/2000, and for some time after that. You need to consult the supplier of the particular system and those responsible for the integration of the larger system. They in turn may need to consult their suppliers. Note that in these cases attention needs to be paid (1) to the components of the particular system, (2) to the system as a unit, and (3) to the larger system of which it is a part. This is because although each part may function correctly when examined separately this is not a guarantee that the whole will work properly when the parts are assembled into a device or system.

### Computer systems used in manufacturing or process control

This relates to cases where the computer is connected to plant, machinery or equipment in order to control it. This includes automated logistics/storage and delivery systems. These systems are liable to be affected in exactly the same way as commercial data processing systems, because the hardware and the systems software are the same, and because the applications software may have been developed along similar lines. Note also that there is a developing trend to link process control with business systems (for example to enable sales figures and stock levels to determine automatically which quantities of which products should be produced). This means that there is the possibility of knock-on effects from one to the other. In these instances it is probable that enquiries need to begin in-house with the engineers and the IT departments, or, if appropriate, the facilities manager. There are also off-the-shelf hardware/ software packages which fall into this category; in their case the supplier needs to be consulted.

### Categorization in relation to checking

In relation to possible actions, there are two distinct categories of embedded systems:

■ Those based on a "normal" computer where the software can be examined or modified. In some cases, only the supplier of the hardware or system and not the user company may be able to make modifications; and

■ Those whose software is inaccessible and/or cannot be modified. This includes (a) items where the software is embedded as firmware and (b) items where it may be physically possible to access the software but impractical to modify it because of the form in which it is written. In either case there are almost certainly instances where the hardware used is not the hardware specified or where the embedded software is different from the software as originally specified.

Software may need to be considered in three categories with regard to modification:

■ Systems software supplied by the computer manufacturer, where modification by you may invalidate the terms of your contract with the supplier;

■ Software supplied by a third party. Modification of code in a shrink-wrapped package may invalidate the terms and conditions of the sale. Conversely, if you have accepted custom-made software from a supplier who no longer has any maintenance obligations, you are likely to be able to modify it. However, if extensive modifications have been made, it may be more difficult to persuade the supplier to accept a new contract for further modifications; and

■ Software developed in-house for which you have responsibility.

## Embedded systems: application categories

### Multi-loop control and monitoring

DCS, SCADA, telemetry

### Panel mounted devices

Control, display, recording and operations

## Safety and security

Alarm and trip systems, fire and gas systems, buildings and facilities security.

## Field devices

Measurement, actuation

## Analytical systems

Laboratory systems; online/ plant systems

## Electrical supply

Supply, measurement, control, protection

## Tools

For design, documentation, testing, maintenance.

Reproduced by permission of The Institution of Electrical Engineers from their Web site at http://www.iee.org.uk/2000risk/

IEE also publish *Embedded Systems and the Year 2000*.


## Checklist

Here is a list of some of the systems that might have embedded microcontrollers. Get back to the manufacturers (suppliers may not have enough information) and get written confirmation from senior (technical) management as to the problems that might arise, if any, on the turn of the century or any other date-related problems (e.g., does "00" — or any other specific characters — in the date field cause the system to fail or the process to abort?). Do not get verbal assurances, and (regrettably) do not rely on the words of sales or marketing personnel.

## Office systems and mobile equipment

- ☐ Answering machines
- ☐ Copiers
- ☐ Desktop computers
- ☐ Faxes
- ☐ Laptops and notebooks
- ☐ Mobile telephones
- ☐ PD's, Personal organizers
- ☐ Still and video cameras
- ☐ Telephone systems
- ☐ Time recording systems
- ☐ Voice mail

## Building systems

- ☐ Air conditioning
- ☐ Backup lighting and generators
- ☐ Building management
- ☐ Burglar and fire alarms
- ☐ CCTV systems
- ☐ Door locks
- ☐ Fire control systems
- ☐ Heating and ventilating systems
- ☐ Lifts, elevators, escalators
- ☐ Lighting systems
- ☐ Safes and vaults
- ☐ Security access control systems
- ☐ Security systems
- ☐ Security cameras
- ☐ Sprinkler systems
- ☐ Switching systems

## Manufacturing and process control

- ☐ Automated factories
- ☐ Bottling plants
- ☐ CAD systems
- ☐ Energy control systems
- ☐ Manufacturing plants
- ☐ Nuclear power stations

☐ Oil refineries/storage facilities

☐ Power grid systems

☐ Power stations

☐ Robots

☐ Switching systems

☐ Water and sewage systems

☐ Time/clock stamps

## Transport

☐ Airplanes (air control, avionics, cabin systems, electrical, flight systems, mechanical/hydraulic and propulsion)

☐ Air traffic control systems

☐ Automobiles

☐ Baggage handling

☐ Buses

☐ Car parking and other meters

☐ Check-in

☐ Command/control systems

☐ Emergency equipment

☐ Jetties

☐ Marine craft

☐ Photo surveillance systems

☐ Radar systems

☐ Signaling systems

☐ Speed cameras/radar detectors

☐ Ticketing systems/ machines

☐ Traffic lights

☐ Trains

☐ Passenger information systems

## Communications

☐ Telephone exchanges

☐ Cable systems

☐ Telephone switches

☐ Satellites

## Banking and finance

☐ Automated teller systems   ☐ Credit card systems

## Medical

☐ Imaging equipment   ☐ Medical equipment

☐ Building facilities

## Domestic equipment

## Catering Equipment

## Central heating control

## VCRs

# Appendix Seven

## Retail Checklist

The National Retail Federation in the United States has produced a checklist to help its members identify their IT and stores' operation needs for the Year 2000. While this list may be more extensive than a smaller retail operation would require, it gives an insight into the range of areas that must be considered by retailers.

### Business Unit Assessment — Corporate

- Energy Management Systems
- Access Control Systems
- Elevator/Escalator Control Systems
- Alarm Systems
- Time Entry Systems
- Telephone Systems
- Auto Attendant/Voice Mail Systems
- Departmental PC Hardware Inventory
- Departmental PC Software Inventory
- Non-IS Application Inventory

### Business Unit Assessment — Human Resources

- PC, Server, and Network Hardware Inventory

- PC, Server and Network Software Inventory
- Application Inventory

## Business Unit Assessment — Finance

- Financial Planning Calculators
- User Generated Applications, e.g., Focus
- Treasury Application
- Accounts Payable
- Key Data Entry
- Inquiry Reports
- Tax Department
- Loss Prevention

## Business Unit Assessment — Corporate Data Center Requirements

- Energy Management Systems
- Access Control Systems
- Alarm Systems
- Time Entry Systems
- Water Cooling and Control Systems
- UPS/UBS Control/Alarm System
- Host Hardware Inventory
- Communications Component Inventory and Control Systems
- System Software Inventory
- Application Software Inventory

## Business Unit Assessment — Store Operations

- Macintosh — e.g., Plan-A-Gram System
- Advertising

- Macintosh — Advertising System
- Imaging System(s)
- Ad Preparation Equipment/System

## Business Unit Assessment — Stores; All Stand-Alone Facilities

- Energy Management Systems
- Access Control Systems
- Alarm Systems
- Time Entry Systems
- Vault/Safe Equipment and/or Systems
- POS PC, Server and Network Hardware Inventory
- Scanners
- Time Entry Equipment/System
- Telephone System
- Auto Attendant/Voice Mail Systems
- Elevator/Escalator Control Systems
- Repair or Analyze Equipment
- Non-POS PC, Server, and Network Hardware Inventory

## Business Unit Assessment — Distribution Centers, ALL

- Energy Management, Alarm Systems, etc.
- Time Entry Equipment/Systems
- Telephone Systems
- Auto Attendant/Voice Mail Systems
- PC, Server, and Network Hardware Inventory
- Sanitation Equipment
- Fashion/Garment Sorters
- White Carousel

- Hand Held Scanners
- RF Equipment
- Charging Equipment/Systems
- Ticketing Hardware Inventory
- Fuel Dispensing Equipment
- Vault/Safe Equipment and/or Systems

## Business Unit Assessment — Product Services and/or Service Centers

- Product Warranties — Fulfillment
- Identify Year 2000 Noncompliant Products
- Telephone Company System
- Auto Attendant/Voice Mail Systems
- Time Entry Equipment/Systems
- Vault/Safe Equipment and/or Systems
- PC, Server, and Network Hardware Inventory
- PC, Server, and Network Software Inventory

## Business Unit Assessment — Import/Export Offices

- Energy Management, Alarm Systems, Access Systems, etc.
- Time Entry Equipment/Systems
- PC, Server, and Network Hardware Inventory
- PC, Server, and Network Software Inventory
- Telephone System
- Auto Attendant/Voice Mail Systems

# About the authors

## Lynn Craig, B.Sc. (Hons)

Lynn has worked in an IT environment since 1982. She has been responsible for computerizing information flow for a number of projects, the main being the Government's Microelectronics Education Program (1982–86) which provided information on the availability of educational software materials. In 1986 she started up her own business, Creative Data.

Working on the principle that any IT investment can only be successful if it addresses the human and organizational factors involved. Lynn specializes in encouraging small business to exploit the potential — and to be prepared for the problems — of new technology.

Honorary Vice-Chairman of the North-East Region of the Federation of Small Businesses in the United Kingdom.

## Mike Kusmirak, LL.B., F.C.A.

Mike has run a number of small- and medium-sized enterprises technology (a service bureau, a hardware manufacturer, a software distributor and a maintenance company).

He is currently involved in online publishing ventures, and works with the public sector on improving the flow of information from Government to the public. In 1995, following discussion with public sector users, he established the Computer Information Center to publish various IT directories. These are now online at http://www.compinfo.co.uk, which currently attracts more than half a million visitors annually.

# Index